Practical
Project
Management

Practical Project Management

*The Secrets of Managing
Any Project on Time
and on Budget*

Michael Dobson

SkillPath Publications
Mission, KS

Editor: Kelly Scanlon

Page Layout and Cover Design: Rod Hankins

ISBN: 1-57294-015-8

Library of Congress Catalog Card Number: 96-67864

10   06

Printed in the United States of America

For my beloved wife and partner

Deborah Singer Dobson

Contents

What Is a Project?

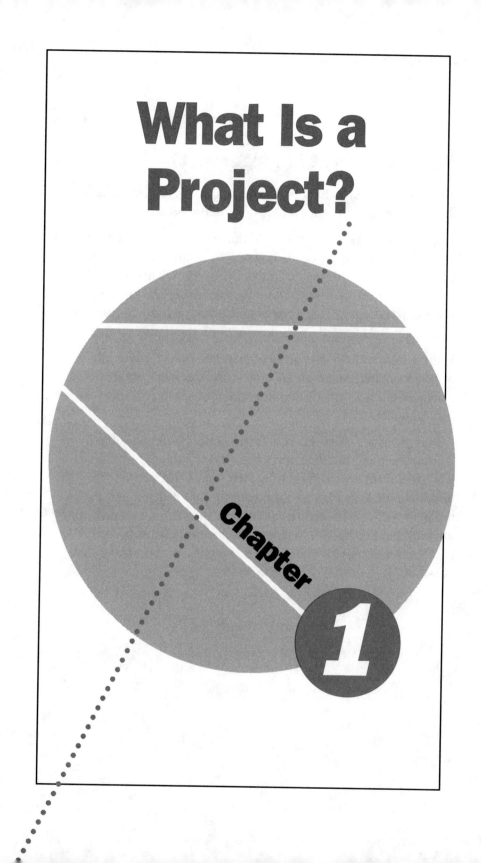

Chapter

1

What Is Project Management?

The most important thing to know about project management is that first and foremost *it's a way of thinking about projects.*

Project management is not simply drawing charts, or using project management software, or leading teams, or any of the rest of the technical material presented in this book. The charts, the software, the teams, and everything else are means to an end: *helping you control your projects to achieve your goals*—on time, on budget, and according to performance standards.

There is no virtue in preparing a chart for its own sake. The tools of project management aren't project management. Project management is a way of thinking; the tools help you carry out that thinking.

Project managers have been defined as people responsible for doing something that has never been done before, for people who don't know what they want, who must first predict the unknown, make a plan to cope with the unforeseen, and execute the plan with too-limited resources that they do not control, and who are held completely responsible for the results, even if miracles are required. This book is designed to help make that possible.

Quiz

Answer the following questions "T" for "True" or "F" for "False."

T   F

☐   ☐   My boss always gives me all the money I need to get my projects done the right way.

☐   ☐   My boss always gives me all the time I need to get my projects done the right way.

☐   ☐   My boss always gives me all the people and resources I need to get my projects done the right way.

☐   ☐   My boss always gives me enough authority to get my projects done the right way.

☐   ☐   My bosses and customers always know what they want the project to accomplish, and they state it clearly.

If you answered "false" to nearly all these questions, you're a normal project manager.

How Projects Differ From "Normal" Work

A project is something that's distinct from the normal circumstances of everyday work. A project has the following characteristics:

1. A project is goal oriented.

A project has a beginning, a middle, and most of all, an end. The goal behind any project is to achieve some defined result. A project is never simply an end in itself; rather it is a means to an end.

Project: Build a new warehouse

Not a Project: Get the accounting reports done each month

Project: Publish the June issue of the employee newsletter

Not a Project: Decide which work assignments have priority

2. A project consists of tasks that can be put into a connected and interrelated sequence.

A key element of projects is that they can be broken down into tasks, which are the specific work packages that have to be accomplished in order to achieve the goal. In an important sense, there is really no such thing as project management; rather, there is task management. From a technical perspective, when you manage a project, you break the project down into tasks, organize the tasks into a logical order (a "plan"), and manage the performance of the tasks, one by one. If you've broken down the tasks properly and you manage each one successfully, your project's outcome should be fairly certain.

So, the concept of "tasks" makes project management possible.

3. A project has a limited duration.

Because projects have specific goals and a plan for achieving them, projects are always and necessarily time-limited. If the project seems never to approach an actual conclusion, one of two things is true:

1. It wasn't really a project in the first place, but rather a program.

2. It's a project, but one that's in serious trouble. The goal of project management is ultimately to end the project, preferably successfully.

4. A project is unique and nonroutine.

If you do it all the time, and it's the primary activity or at least one of the primary activities of your job, it's not really a project.

With a project, you are trying to achieve a specific goal. Once the project is complete, you shouldn't have to do that specific project again.

Each project has unique problems and situations. Some projects are unique in every respect. Others are similar in topic, but unique in their details. For example, a book publisher publishes many books. Each book is a project because it has a goal, it can be broken into tasks, and the process of publishing the book is limited. When the book is published, that specific project is completed, and the published book is the project outcome. That book doesn't need to be published again. Marketing the book is more appropriately considered a program, because it's ongoing (see "Projects Versus Programs Versus Priorities"). While a book may go out of print at some point, that point is not predetermined, and the publisher (not to mention the author) normally wants to delay that event as long as possible.

Even though all book publishing projects are similar, each individual book project has its unique qualities. Books differ in topic, page count, format, illustrations, target audience, and many other features. As you can see, some parts of managing book projects are the same, but each individual book differs in at least some respects.

In other words, there are no "cookie cutter" projects. If you are managing similar projects, take advantage of the similarities to streamline the planning and management process, but be sure to plan for the differences and issues that make each project unique.

Projects Versus Programs Versus Priorities

The first question in project management is always, "Do you have a project to manage?" Many normal management functions, even quite complex and important ones, aren't projects. They simply don't fit the technical definition.

If it's not a project, it may be a *program*. A program has no conclusion; it's ongoing and indefinite. Perhaps one day we'll stop preparing monthly reports, but the aim of the program is to prepare them. There is no end. A program manager's primary duty is to achieve better quality performance (faster, better, cheaper) from the ongoing program. Continuous Improvement (from TQM) processes, which have no definite end, are good examples of programs.

Sometimes, the concern is *priorities management,* or how to separate the merely urgent from the truly important. To manage your priorities, you need to have an overall goal (to lower costs, to grow market share, to make a better automobile) that doesn't have a predetermined end point. You can lower costs forever, at least in theory. You can always make your car better, or at least different. You can always grow market share.

Program management and priorities management, however important to the organization, are not the same thing as project management, which involves nonroutine, goal-oriented projects with limited duration. You can apply many of the tools and ideas of project management to other aspects of your work, but not necessarily all of them.

Why You Don't Get the Money, Time, or People You Need

The very characteristics of a project help explain why it sometimes seems that senior management sits up late at night thinking of new ways to stick it to your projects. They do, you see, because that's their job—really!

Remember that in every organization, there are far more projects that are desirable and potentially profitable than there are resources to manage them. In other words, work is infinite but resources are finite.

Every time senior management gives you a dollar for your project, every time they give you a person for your project, every time they give you a week for your project, that is a dollar, a person, or a week they can't give to someone else running a different project that also has value.

Why don't you get the authority you need? Again, because projects are time-limited and unique. Every project manager would like to control purchasing, for example, or data processing. Yet if there are multiple projects going on in a company, not every project manager can control these *common* areas. Sometimes you need resources or people for part of your project, and others need the same resources or people for part of their projects. Getting all the authority you need would either deprive other project managers or require redoing the entire table of organization for each project—or both. It's not practical.

You must always plan on managing your projects in an environment of scarcity and authority limits because senior management can't give you everything you might want—and simultaneously achieve their other goals.

How to Train an Elephant

("Orange Ropes")

To train an elephant, always start with a baby elephant. Get a length of strong rope, and paint it bright orange. Tie the orange rope around the leg of the baby elephant. The baby elephant will not like this, and will try to escape. The orange rope is too strong for the elephant, who eventually gives up.

If you use the orange rope technique long enough, the baby elephant grows to adulthood. Now, take any rope, no matter how rotten or flimsy, and paint it bright orange, just as before. Tie the orange rope around the leg of the giant, full-grown elephant, and the elephant cannot escape. The elephant looks at the orange rope and thinks: "Hmm... orange rope. I know from experience that you can't break an orange rope."

Moral: You have real barriers and real problems in managing your projects, but some are simply "orange ropes." There's only one way to break an orange rope—to recognize it for what it truly is and overcome the "restraint."

The Project Life Cycle—A Process Map for Your Success

Baseball great Yogi Berra warned, "If you don't know where you're going, you just might end up somewhere else."

Part of thinking like a project manager involves knowing where you're going—understanding the life cycle of a project (see fig. 1.1). The key lesson of the project life cycle is this: *each step depends on its predecessor.* To manage your project successfully, do the work in this order:

Define. Before you can ever do a competent job managing a project, you must first define what you're doing and why. Success expert Brian Tracy calls goal setting "the threshold skill underlying all achievement." Nowhere is this more true than in the area of projects. While a good goal will not guarantee a successful project, the lack of a good goal guarantees failure.

The new Denver International Airport was run by highly experienced and intelligent project managers, and nevertheless ended up behind schedule, over budget, and unable to achieve its performance objectives. Why? One key reason may be that the project originators and management did not fully define what they wanted to achieve before they went to work. Project goals continued to evolve during the actual work, forcing expensive re-dos, abrupt changes in direction and, ultimately, public embarrassment.

The failure to define properly is the single biggest cause of project failure.

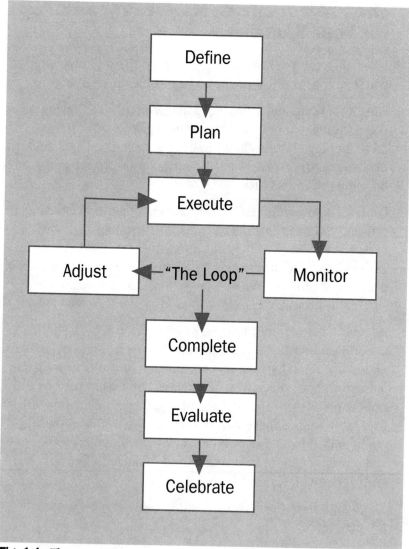

Fig. 1.1. *The project life cycle.*

Plan. Planning is the technical heart of the discipline known as project management. From Gantt charts to PERT and CPM, from Work Breakdown Structures to budgets, good project managers plan thoroughly. Planning has two major virtues:

1. A good plan teaches you about your project.

2. Any plan, whether good or not, helps you monitor where your project is, compared to where it should be.

"The Loop." Once you have your plan in place, you're ready to begin the actual management of your project. This process is called "the Loop" because it contains the three steps you repeat in sequence throughout the management phase until your project is complete. The three elements of the Loop are:

1. **Execute.** This is the process of assigning tasks to team members and ensuring that they carry out the work.

2. **Monitor.** Compare the tasks being completed to the plan. Is the work being completed on time, on budget, and according to performance specifications?

3. **Adjust.** Whenever monitoring reveals a discrepancy between plan and reality, it's time to make adjustments. The earlier you find a problem, the easier it is to solve.

The Godzilla Principle

In Japanese monster movies, there's frequently a scene where the monster *du jour* (Godzilla, Mothra, Gamora, etc.) is a cute little baby monster. People say, "Oh, what a cute little monster!" Obviously, there's no urgency. They ignore the monster.

They wait until the monster is full grown and busily stomping downtown Tokyo, and then they shout, "What are we going to do?"

The answer is, of course, nothing. When Godzilla is rampaging through downtown Tokyo, there's very little you can do about it. The best option has passed.

On your projects, spend time in "baby monster patrol." Every time you find a little problem with the power to grow into a big one later, stomp on it at once.

For example, imagine that you're in charge of your company's summer picnic. Consider:

- Could it rain on your picnic?

- Can you predict whether it will?

- Can you control whether it will?

- Will your boss let you off the hook if it does rain?

Do you think it's fair to be held responsible for something you can neither predict nor control?

Well it is fair, because you aren't helpless. There are at least three quick solutions:

1. A rain date

2. A rented tent

3. A location with an indoor pavilion

Notice that if you use any of these solutions, whether it rains is no longer an issue. If, however, it never occurs to you that it might rain on your picnic, you obviously won't plan for the possibility and on the morning of the picnic when it's raining cats and dogs, you'll be looking out the window and frantically thinking, "Now what?"

Godzilla has entered Tokyo.

Complete. It may seem like an exercise in the blindingly obvious to point this step out, but a project isn't finished until it's complete. Nevertheless, in many organizations numerous projects litter the halls, 90 percent complete, and have been for some time, yet no one can seem to get them finished. You may be wondering why make a fuss about some unfinished projects—if they're not being worked on, there's no current expenditure, right? Wrong. These projects consume opportunity costs and morale dollars merely by existing. Finish them or shoot them— there's no happy medium.

The final two stages of a project have more to do with the next project than the current one, but they're still vital.

Evaluate. The savvy project manager always evaluates each project, not to fault-find, but rather to gain wisdom for the future.

What went wrong? How could we have anticipated it better? How could we have handled it better? What surprises did we encounter? Could they have been predicted? What went right that we might have taken better advantage of?

Write this information down and use it to improve the success of future projects. You'll be a better project manager for it.

Celebrate. *The One-Minute Manager* author Ken Blanchard says, "The number one job of management is appreciation." People work for appreciation; they care about being part of a winning team. Always take the time to spread the praise around, to provide appropriate rewards or mementos, to write commendation memos, and above all, to say a simple but honest "thank you." People make your projects successful; you owe them for that. When you pay this debt of honor, people will be far more willing to work for you in the future. That's a project management asset that will benefit you forever.

How to Create a "Miracle on Demand"

Experienced project managers sometimes look like miracle workers. They bring in a project that seems impossible, and solve problems that others can't. They have learned to think like project managers—and to use the tools of project management effectively. As you read and practice the tools provided in this book, you'll learn some of the secrets for looking like a miracle worker yourself.

Here are four of them:

1. Your projects are full of hidden resources and opportunities.

Every project has hidden resources that can solve many of your problems. Proper planning will help you uncover those resources and use them properly. These resources go by strange names—resource slack, weak constraint flexibility, control point identification. You'll learn how to uncover and use them as you read this book.

Resources are scarce—so don't waste the ones you have. Remember: You waste a resource if you don't know it's there in the first place.

2. When you need *one* great idea, start with *several* ideas.

The tools of brainstorming are an important resource for project managers. Don't go it alone; get input and fresh ideas from other sources. When you're overstressed and over-anxious, racing your brain for insights and solutions, you don't think at top capacity. Allow your project team to carry some of the creative load; it helps you—and it improves their morale at the same time.

3. Take the time to plan and to set goals.

Thousands of projects fail each year because their managers didn't do the preliminary steps in the right order, especially defining and planning. Make sure you know what the goal of the project is; make sure you understand the work; make sure you have a plan. Then start the work. You wouldn't go to target practice and shout, "Ready! Fire! Aim!" Don't take that attitude with your projects.

4. Use the Godzilla principle.

Brainstorm to find *potential* problems—and act on them now. Use the Monitor stage to scout continually for embryonic disasters. Design early warning systems and event triggers to help you plan. To solve any problem more easily, catch it early.

Exercise #1:

Looking Back

To prepare for your next project, write an evaluation of the last project you worked on—whether you completed it or not. Answer the following questions as you write. If you respond "no" to any question, explain why and jot down what you can do to avoid this pitfall on your next project.

1. Did you have a clear idea of what the project was supposed to accomplish?

   ☐ Yes   ☐ No

   _____

   _____

   _____

   _____

   _____

   _____

2. Did you identify the customers and originators of the project and determine what exactly they wanted, needed, and expected?

   ☐ Yes   ☐ No

   _____

   _____

   _____

   _____

   _____

   _____

3. Did you have clear knowledge of the resources available to you and what their limits were?

☐ Yes   ☐ No

_____

_____

_____

_____

_____

_____

4. Was your project segmented into tasks that were the right size for people to manage and execute?

☐ Yes   ☐ No

_____

_____

_____

_____

_____

_____

5. Did you have a written plan?

☐ Yes   ☐ No

_____

_____

_____

_____

_____

_____

6. Did you get input and involvement from project team members in the planning stages?

☐ Yes   ☐ No

_____

_____

_____

_____

_____

7. Were your team members committed to the project goals?

☐ Yes   ☐ No

_____

_____

_____

_____

_____

8. Were you able to build consensus and effective agreement among your team members?

☐ Yes   ☐ No

_____

_____

_____

_____

_____

9. Were the members of your team cooperative in following your requests?

☐ Yes ☐ No

_____

_____

_____

_____

_____

_____

10. Were you able to motivate your team to be creative and effective?

☐ Yes ☐ No

_____

_____

_____

_____

_____

_____

11. Did you get the job done?

☐ Yes ☐ No

_____

_____

_____

_____

_____

_____

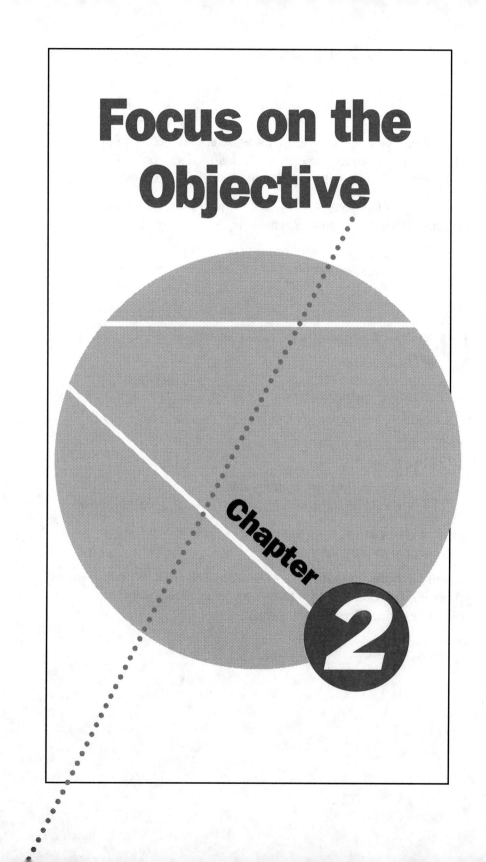

Focus on the Objective

Chapter

2

The military genius Karl von Clausewitz reminds us, "This above all: the principle of the objective." To manage any project successfully, you must be absolutely clear about the objective.

More projects fail because they lack fully and correctly defined objectives than for any other reason.

Take the simple quiz that follows to see if you have an "objectives definition" problem.

 *uiz*

1. Can you define your project objective right now in twenty-five words or less? ☐ Yes ☐ No

2. Can you list all the potential customers of this project? ☐ Yes ☐ No

3. Do your projects avoid frequent last-minute change orders? ☐ Yes ☐ No

4. Do you know what the project is designed to improve for your customers? ☐ Yes ☐ No

If you have any "no" answers, you may have an objectives problem. Read on to find out how to define your project objectives and solve problems early.

The Importance of Defining Project Goals and Objectives

A *goal* is a change that one or more customers desire. Goals can involve cost savings, revenue improvements, work process improvements, saving time, and so on.

An *objective* is a written statement of a project, designed to achieve one or more goals.

Often, the process of defining goals and objectives is complex and political. Too many project managers, especially those who come from the technical ranks where facts count more than feelings and competency is respected above all, find themselves short-circuiting the defining process and going right to work. This is a critical mistake. *If you achieve the wrong goal, no matter how brilliantly you do so, your project is a failure.*

Let's go through the goal-setting process the right way, using a real project from history.

The year: 1961

The place: Washington, D.C.

Your job: Administrator, National Aeronautics and Space Administration

As a Washington big-shot in 1961, you have a nice office overlooking the Mall. You even have your own office television set. Your secretary comes in to announce, "The President's on TV." You turn on the television, because you know the speech involves NASA. During President John Kennedy's speech, you hear, "We commit this nation to put a man on the moon and return him safely to this earth by the end of this decade, and to do the other things, not because they are easy but because they are hard."

The applause rings out. You, however, feel a mixture of anticipation and dread. You've just received a project assignment.

What now?

Always begin the process of setting a project objective by defining the Triple Constraints.

Triple Constraints are the key elements in any project definition. You must fully define and understand the Triple Constraints before you begin to manage any project. The three constraints are:

- **Time constraint:** How long do you have?

- **Budget constraint:** How much can you spend?

- **Performance criteria:** What results must your project achieve to meet its purpose?

Nine Steps for Using the Triple Constraints to Define Your Project and Solve Problems Early

Understanding how to use the Triple Constraints is essential to becoming an effective project manager. On the surface, this seems like an exercise in the blindingly obvious. Of course, you need to know time, budget, and performance standards. Yet as you delve into the Moon Project, you'll discover just how much rich and insightful information examining the Triple Constraints can yield. The rest of this chapter discusses the nine steps involved in using the Triple Constraints to define your project.

Nine Steps to Defining Your Project

Step 1: Identify the key project participants.

Step 2: Define the "rough draft" constraints.

Step 3: Analyze missing constraints.

Step 4: Identify preliminary management issues.

Step 5: Examine the Triple Constraints to set priorities.

Step 6: Use the project goal to make the constraints more exact.

Step 7: Identify secondary and tertiary project goals—and who wants them.

Step 8: Refine your project goals and test them with the affected parties.

Step 9: Use the Triple Constraints regularly throughout the project to help you solve problems and meet challenges.

Step 1: Identify the key project participants. Your first insight is that there are, so far, two participants on this project: (1) you, the project manager, and (2) President Kennedy, the project originator. In rare cases, the project manager may originate his or her own project, but usually the role of the project manager is that of a hired hand. You are hired to do what the project originator wants. The originator may be your boss, your boss's boss, or an outside customer. Often, there are multiple project originators, each with their own pet agendas. (You'll learn how to deal with that situation later.)

Step 2: Define the "rough draft" constraints. From Kennedy's speech, you know some things about the Triple Constraints already:

Project: Put a man on the moon

Time constraint: By the end of the decade

Performance criteria: Safe return to Earth

Notice that the project would have been much faster and cheaper had it involved a one-way trip, but it wouldn't have achieved the right objective. Saving money and saving time are important, but not the only criteria.

Budget constraint: Unknown and unspecified

Step 3: Analyze missing constraints. Even though the Budget constraint is unspecified, there's *always* a Budget constraint. First, let's explore why the Budget constraint hasn't been specified yet.

The first possible reason is that Kennedy himself didn't have much of an idea what it would cost to go to the moon. This is likely true, and it isn't a criticism of Kennedy. After all, you're the head of NASA, the technical expert. Project originators often must hire project managers who have the knowledge they themselves lack. You must make up the budget proposal.

Here's a key to your success: Before you can do a good job as a project manager, you have an earlier job, that of project *consultant.* You must advise the project originators on the best way for *them* to achieve *their* goals. Only when you reach consensus can you sensibly move on.

Step 4: Identify preliminary management issues. Two factors drive your initial budget projection. The first is the *technical* challenge. No one has been to the moon yet. Although you are the unquestioned technical expert, you can't know it all. You can only guess at some of the technical challenges you face. Therefore, your budget projection will necessarily contain a large estimating error. NASA professionals call this process a "WAG," short for "Wildly Aimed Guess." As you refine your WAG, it becomes a SWAG ("Scientific Wildly Aimed Guess"). There's nothing wrong with WAGs or SWAGs. Sometimes, they're necessary.

The second factor driving the budget projection is *political.* You can only spend as much as Congress will appropriate for the project. Should you consider political realities yourself, or delegate that part upward to President Kennedy? The project management answer is clear:

Never forget to consider political and organizational issues in formulating your objective. Failure to do so will inevitably result in change orders later in your project.

So far, the Triple Constraints read as follows:

Project: Put a man on the moon

Time constraint: By the end of the decade

Performance criteria: Safe return to Earth

Budget constraint: What is technically necessary, but no more than Congress is likely to approve

Step 5: Examine the Triple Constraints to set priorities. In the real world, the Triple Constraints are never absolutely identical in priority. There are trade-offs. The old joke goes like this: "You can have it fast, you can have it cheap, or you can have it good. Pick any two."

Although as quality-conscious professionals, project managers want to achieve the best possible goal, they must sometimes make compromises. You must determine which compromises are least damaging to the project.

The first constraint you will identify is the *weak constraint.* (On a different project, you might find a different constraint easier to define first.) The weak constraint is the Triple Constraint that is (a) most flexible and/or (b) least important to achieving your project goal.

First, look for flexibility. Which of the Triple Constraints is most flexible for the Moon Project?

- *Time:* While there is some flexibility on the front-end (you can reach the moon earlier than the end of the decade), there is no flexibility for lateness.

- *Performance:* It's hard to be flexible with "return safely." The astronauts either do or they don't.

- *Budget:* You already know that the technical budget proposal is a SWAG at best; plus there is flexibility in the Congressional budget process.

Budget, therefore, is the weak constraint.

The second way to look for the weak constraint is to look for the least important constraint.

Time: Kennedy was emphatic about the project deadline, and some political issues seem to be at stake.

Performance: Having the astronauts survive the trip is clearly important.

Budget: Does a billion dollars more or less really matter on a program of this scope?

Again, Budget is the weak constraint.

The second constraint you will identify is the driver. The *driver* is the Triple Constraint that drives the project. If you fail to accomplish the driver, the project is a failure, regardless of how well you accomplish the other constraints.

Imagine for a moment that General Schwartzkopf came marching back from the Persian Gulf and went to see President Bush. "Mr. President," he says, "I'm really sorry I lost that war for you. But in my defense, I did it ahead of schedule and way under budget."

You can picture the response. In this project, the driver was clearly Performance.

In the Moon Project, the answer may not be so obvious. Try the following quiz to see if you can identify the driver.

Of the three constraints, which will you select as the driver? Check the correct answer.

☐ A. Time constraint

☐ B. Performance criteria

☐ C. Budget constraint

Obviously, "C" is wrong because it's already been defined as the weak constraint. Most people choose "B," Performance. After all, getting the astronauts safely back to Earth seems very important.

What's the right answer? Actually, it's "D," none of the above. This is a trick question, but it leads to the next insight you must have to be an effective project manager:

The project manager doesn't determine the ranking of the constraints. The project originator and the project goal do.

In other words, you must be careful about jumping to conclusions here. You must determine what the project originator thinks as well as what the ultimate project goal requires.

How will you find out what President Kennedy thinks?

The first way to discover the driver is to ask—but be careful how you ask. Don't say: "Hey, boss! On that new project, did you want it fast, cheap, or good?" The answer will almost always be "All three! Now, get back to work!"

Be more subtle. One technique that may help you is the "forced-choice" question. To do this, offer a hypothetical situation that forces a choice among two of the objectives and ask for the originator's preferred approach.

"Mr. President," you might begin, "as you know, it's impossible to eliminate all risk on something as complex as a moon shot. What if we had these two choices? First, that we go ahead and make the moon shot before the end of the decade with a 60 percent chance of getting the astronauts back alive. Second, we could delay the moon shot until, say, 1972 and by doing so get the safety chance up to 90 percent? If this were the case, which choice would you want us to make?"

This is a perfectly fair question, although you may not always get a straight answer. If you do get a straight answer, it will normally tell you what the driver is. For example, the President might say, "Well, you can't make an omelet without breaking eggs. Let's get there ASAP." Then the driver is Time. Or, the President might say: "We just can't take the political hit from casualties. Be careful out there." Then the driver is Performance.

Once you know the driver, you can design your project around that as your Number One priority.

If you don't get a straight answer, look to the overall project goal. Let's put the space program in its historical context. The primary reason for making the space program the national priority it became had to do with the Cold War. Imagine that Apollo 11 had landed after the Soviets had reached the moon. You could make it before the end of the decade but after the Soviet Union—but you know that wouldn't have been good enough. The United States had to beat the Soviet Union; therefore, the driver had to be Time. Performance criteria became the middle constraint.

The *middle constraint* is the Triple Constraint that is stronger than the weak constraint and weaker than the driver. It comes in the middle.

Does this mean that the United States was prepared to risk astronaut lives to get to the moon first? The historical answer was an unqualified yes. Astronaut safety was important, but getting there before the Soviets was even more important. How much the project cost came third.

The revised Triple Constraints for the project now read like this:

Project: Put a man on the moon

Time constraint: By the end of the decade

Performance criteria: Safe return to Earth

Budget constraint: By spending what is technically necessary, but no more than Congress is likely to approve

Driver: Time constraint

Middle constraint: Performance criteria

Weak constraint: Budget constraint

Can the Triple Constraints change during a project? Yes, but rarely. If your Triple Constraints seem to change on a daily basis, this normally means that you haven't properly defined them in the first place. Sometimes it's hard to pin people down, but you must. Get the Triple Constraints wrong, and everything else in your project will suffer.

Major organizational changes often produce changes in the Triple Constraints.

For example, after the success of the Apollo mission, NASA's organizational culture continued to rank the Triple Constraints in their "traditional" order of time/performance/budget, although the rationale for this order had vanished with the success of the lunar mission. NASA didn't fully integrate a change until the *Challenger* disaster. Even then, Performance criteria didn't become the new driver. Instead, the negative press coverage of NASA (as well as the Hubble telescope debacle) resulted in elevating Budget from

weak constraint to driver, making Performance the middle constraint and Time the new weak constraint. The lack of a deadline for the space station, the new NASA project, is the practical result.

Step 6: Use the project goal to make the constraints more exact. If you take on faith that your project originators always tell you exactly and completely what they wish from you, you're likely running your project into trouble. One of the results of examining the goal that underlies the Moon Project is gaining this insight: When President Kennedy said that the goal was "to put a man on the moon by the end of this decade," he wasn't being totally accurate. If the true goal was to beat the Soviet Union to the moon, the Time constraint should read: "By the end of the decade or before the Soviet Union, whichever comes first."

If you find that management or your customers often pull the rug out from under your projects by shoving change orders down your throat, this may be your problem.

Remember, you're rated by what your project originators and/or customers meant to say, not merely by what they *actually* said. Never take any project assignment at face value. Dig deep to find the real story.

It doesn't matter why the project originator may not state the goal completely. Perhaps President Kennedy thought it was too obvious to state. Perhaps he thought it would be poor diplomacy to say it. No matter the reason, you are still responsible for it. Knowing this will help you avoid numerous last-minute change orders.

An estimated 50 percent of all last-minute project change orders result from factors the project manager either knew or could have known at the beginning of the project. You must control the controllable to have any hope of dealing with the uncontrollable.

For example, on the Moon Project, the most likely single cause of a change order would be a speed-up in the Soviet space program, since the goal is to get there first. Imagine yourself standing in front of the President and saying: "But you told me I had until the end of the decade! It's not fair to make me speed up at this late date!"

Once you've figured out the real objective, you know that it's possible that the project originator will change the deadline for the project based on what the Soviets do. This is critical information. Use it. For example, spend some of your budget on spies. You'd better know more about what's going on in the Soviet space program than the President does. After all, it's your job. There are no excuses.

When the President calls to say, "The CIA just told me the Soviets are going into high gear on their moon program," you need to be able to reply, "Mr. President, I've known that for six months now and I've already initiated the schedule changes to get there first!"

Congratulations! You're now on the way to being a Project Management Hero.

Step 7: Identify secondary and tertiary project goals—and who wants them. The larger your project, the more likely it will affect different people with different interests. This is the reason all projects are political in nature. Different interests generally conflict. In the Moon Project, while "beat the Soviets" was the Number One goal, there were many others.

Many NASA installations were located in the South. Why? Because many powerful members of Congress were from the South. During the Manhattan Project to build the first atomic bomb, President Roosevelt called in a key Tennessee congressman known for putting his district first. Because FDR needed his vote, he spoke persuasively and at length about how the national interest required the congressman's support. The congressman nodded. "Mr. President," he said, "I agree that this is absolutely vital and you have my utmost support. I only have one question. Where exactly in Tennessee do you think we should place this project?"

Besides regional economic issues, there was (and is) a constituency for pure science and space exploration. Although this constituency was not large enough to affect Congress, notice that many NASA employees and contractors joined because of their personal belief and passion for space exploration.

There was also a press and public relations issue. There were complaints about spending money on space exploration when there were pressing local needs. There were egos to soothe. In other words, the Moon Project was just like any other project— only more so.

Make a list of other goals, who has those goals, and what it would take to meet those goals. Notice that some people may have a goal that's incompatible with your project, just like those who felt that spending any money on space exploration was wasteful. Be on the lookout for any constituency devoted to keeping your project from success and, early on, try to anticipate and deal with the obstacles they may present.

First, interview people with disparate goals. Sometimes it's possible to achieve their goals along with the main project goals with no extra cost and time. Wouldn't it be a shame and a waste to have problems from these people when they could so easily have been avoided? A computer firm once installed a $2 million system for a company, and achieved every one of the Triple Constraints. During training, however, they found out that the people who had to operate the system hated it. It didn't do anything they wanted. One of the programmers realized, "If we'd known about their needs, we could have integrated them into our project with no extra cost or time. But we didn't ask."

Second, identify potential conflicts. If you can meet everybody's needs within the same project time and budget, wonderful! If you can't, perhaps you can meet all the needs with extra time and/or extra money. You should at least ask—you just might get the resources, and the organization will benefit.

Third, work with conflicts. If you have needs you can't meet with your resources and no additional resources are available, or if you can't achieve all the goals that your project constituency has, you must make a decision. Use this three-step process:

1. Get the affected parties together to try to achieve their own consensus; act on the consensus. If this fails...

2. Make the decision based on the overall goals of the company to the best of your ability. Get advice from management if you need it. If this fails...

3. Make the decision based on who has the most power to help or hurt you. (Notice that this is not based exclusively on rank. Sometimes the actual users have tremendous power: the power to make the project fail.)

Step 8: Refine your project goals and test them with the affected parties. The final project constraints read as follows:

Project: Put a man on the moon

Time constraint: Before the Soviet Union does, or by the end of the decade, whichever comes first

Performance criteria: Safe return to Earth. Secondary: Provide as much infrastructure for future space exploration as possible. Deliver quality, pure scientific information.

Budget constraint: What is technically necessary, but no more than Congress is likely to approve. Secondary: Emphasize work in key congressional districts and technology spin-offs

Driver: Time constraint

Middle constraint: Performance criteria

Weak constraint: Budget constraint

Step 9: Use the Triple Constraints regularly throughout the project to help you solve problems and meet your challenges. One particular source of power project managers often overlook is the power inherent in the weak constraint. As head of NASA, if you are in trouble on the Time constraint, the first thing you should consider is spending more money. In the current NASA environment, however, the clearest way to meet the Budget driver is to delay the project goal.

In the Persian Gulf War, General Schwartzkopf was faced with a Performance driver and Time as the middle constraint because of the issues of keeping the international alliance and domestic political opinion together. Notice that he brought over far more resources than some thought necessary. He used the flexibility of the weak constraint—a hidden resource for a savvy project manager.

Look Before You Leap

As you can see, much is involved in the definition phase of your project. Many project managers, including some who are very experienced, rush this step or assume they already know what the project is about. Don't fall into this trap, no matter how experienced you get.

Don't rush this phase. The most dangerous words that can ever come out of your mouth as a project manager are, "Yes, I'll do it!" before you truly understand what you've agreed to. When you say "yes," you aren't merely agreeing to what has actually been said, but also to every hidden assumption, wish, and fantasy your project originators may have.

This isn't to suggest that you should say "no," or even that you have the option of saying "no." You can, however, ask questions and dig, all the time making positive noises, up until you're ready to accept the assignment. Will this cause problems with your boss or customer? Not necessarily. Many bosses would have more respect for certain members of their staffs if these people did ask a few more questions at the beginning of a project rather than waiting until disaster strikes.

You may be thinking that this is an enormous amount of work to do just to get the goal right. But consider this: You haven't even begun to plan, much less manage your project. But doing the objective and goal-setting part perfectly is the most critical phase of the project. Do this stage right and everything else will be easier. Do it wrong, and nothing else will save you.

After all, if you don't have time to get it right in the first place, when exactly do you expect to find the time to do it over?

Exercise #2:

Ranking the Triple Constraints

Try identifying and then ranking the Triple Constraints for the following project. The answers are on the next page.

Project: The Smithsonian National Air and Space Museum, the world's most popular museum, was a Federal government project accomplished ahead of schedule and under budget.

The goal of the project was to build a world-class aviation and space museum for a budget of $30 million and open it on July 4, 1976.

1. Identify the Triple Constraints.

   Project: _____

   Performance criteria: _____

   Budget constraint: _____

   Time constraint: _____

2. Rank the Triple Constraints.

   Driver: _____

   Middle constraint: _____

   Weak constraint: _____

Answers to Exercise #2:

1. Identify the Triple constraints

Project:	*National Air and Space Museum*
Performance criteria:	*World-class*
Budget constraint:	*$30 million*
Time constraint:	*July 4, 1976*

2. Rank the Triple Constraints

Driver:	*Time*
Middle constraint:	*Budget*
Weak constraint:	*Performance*

The driver is obviously the Time constraint because the museum was an important part of the bicentennial celebration.

The weak constraint was the Performance criteria. Although "world class" is arguably the most *important* of the constraints, it's equally the most *flexible*. If you've been to the museum, you probably didn't count the number of airplanes on display. Why? Because you didn't care. Your idea of world-class wouldn't have been affected whether there were thirty or forty airplanes hanging; therefore, if problems developed, hanging fewer airplanes might allow the museum to open on time and on budget with insignificant impact on customer perception.

Budget is the middle constraint. Thirty million dollars is a round number. No one expected the project to cost exactly $30,000,000.00. In fact, even plus or minus a few hundred thousand would have been considered "on budget." A $100,000 variance would amount to only ±0.1 percent, pretty good for a project that size.

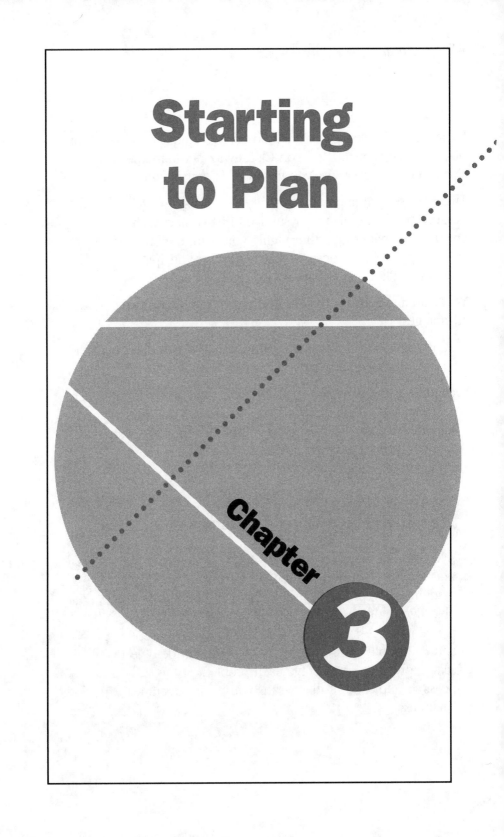

Starting to Plan

Chapter

3

Dwight David Eisenhower once observed, "Plans are useless, but planning is essential." Karl von Clausewitz put it another way: "No battle plan ever survived first contact with the enemy."

There are several important truths here. "Plans are useless" because "no battle plan ever survived first contact with the enemy." No matter how thoroughly you plan, the uniqueness of each project virtually ensures that you won't anticipate everything. Plans never happen exactly as planned.

Yet "planning is essential" because plans provide two key advantages:

First, the process of planning is educational. If you don't make a plan, you don't know what your project is about.

Second, a plan always serves as a benchmark, a way to tell where you are relative to your destination. A roadmap is useful even when you get lost; a project plan is useful even—especially—when your project goes off track.

Transition From Goals to Plans

According to the official process of project management, you must establish an objective before you proceed with the planning process. Realistically, however, the boundaries of objective setting and planning blur. As you work through the planning process, expect to uncover questions, problems, and issues that are best solved by reopening the objective-setting process. Try to solve each problem in the earliest possible step, even if that means you must sometimes backtrack.

From Project Level to Task Level— Stage 1 of Your Plan

The process of planning begins with the project itself. To create a plan, you must break the project down into tasks.

A *task* is a work package that is one element of a larger project. Like a project, a task has a beginning, a middle, and a clearly defined end. Also like a project, a task always has the Triple Constraints of time, budget, and performance.

A *subtask* is a task that is broken down into smaller work packages. Use subtasks to improve detailed control in larger projects where the identified tasks are themselves complex and hard to manage.

A *subproject* is sometimes used as a synonym for "task." A very large project is often broken down into subprojects, which are further broken down into tasks and then into subtasks.

Operationally, whether your work assignment is a project, a subproject, a task, or a subtask depends primarily on your perspective. In other words, where you stand depends on where you sit.

The key to successful task planning is not to forget anything. If you fail to identify all the tasks required to accomplish your project goal, you'll naturally fail to budget time and resources for those tasks. When you discover later that they really do exist and you have to do them anyway, your project is in trouble.

Unless the project is so small and simple that you can guarantee you won't forget anything, use the brainstorming process to identify tasks. Here are the steps:

1. Assemble your project team, or at least key members who represent the different major functional areas of your project.

2. Brainstorm every task you can think of. Write the tasks down on individual "sticky" notes so you can move them around and group them later.

3. Refine your tasks. As your team brainstorms, individual members will think of tasks based on their own conceptions of the project. You may identify several different approaches to take, but you will need to choose one approach. Doing so will eliminate some tasks. Other tasks may be able to be combined into larger tasks. Still other tasks will be best managed by breaking them into smaller tasks. Use your judgment.

4. Identify possible categories you can use to organize the tasks.

5. Group the tasks into those categories. (If you're using sticky notes, you can actually move the notes into categories.)

6. Review the list several times for any tasks you may have forgotten.

7. As you continue with the planning process, be alert for discoveries of forgotten tasks.

8. Review the final plan for logical workflow—and check again for anything you may have forgotten.

Exercise #3:
"Bottom-Up" Task Identification

You can do this exercise as an individual or with a group. Imagine that you're responsible for planning your company's summer picnic. Brainstorm all the tasks you must do.

_____

_____

_____

_____

_____

_____

_____

_____

_____

_____

_____

_____

Note: If you did this as an individual exercise, try it again with a group to see how many more items you can come up with. Check the answer key on the next page for items that others who have completed this exercise frequently forget.

Answers to Exercise #3

Here are the picnic tasks people frequently forget:

- Providing toilet facilities
- Scheduling a rain date
- Providing beverages
- Providing utensils
- Arranging cleanup
- Acquiring cooking supplies
- Buying paper plates

Did you forget any of these? What would be the fate of the picnic if you had?

How to Build a Work Breakdown Structure (WBS)

The Work Breakdown Structure, or WBS, helps you organize your project and its tasks. Here are the levels of the WBS.

1. **State the project.** Your WBS starts with Level 1, which is your project (see fig. 3.1).

2. **Define the subprojects.** Subdivide your project into subprojects, which form Level 2 of the WBS (see fig. 3.2). Subprojects actually help define the management structure of your project in addition to defining categories of tasks. For your subprojects, use the categories you created in the brainstorming process. You could normally manage a project such as the company picnic with a committee structure. Committees might include Food and Beverage, Entertainment, Site Operations, Publicity, and Executive. Each committee can be a subproject, and as you group the individual tasks under each subproject, you can instantly tell from the WBS who is responsible for it.

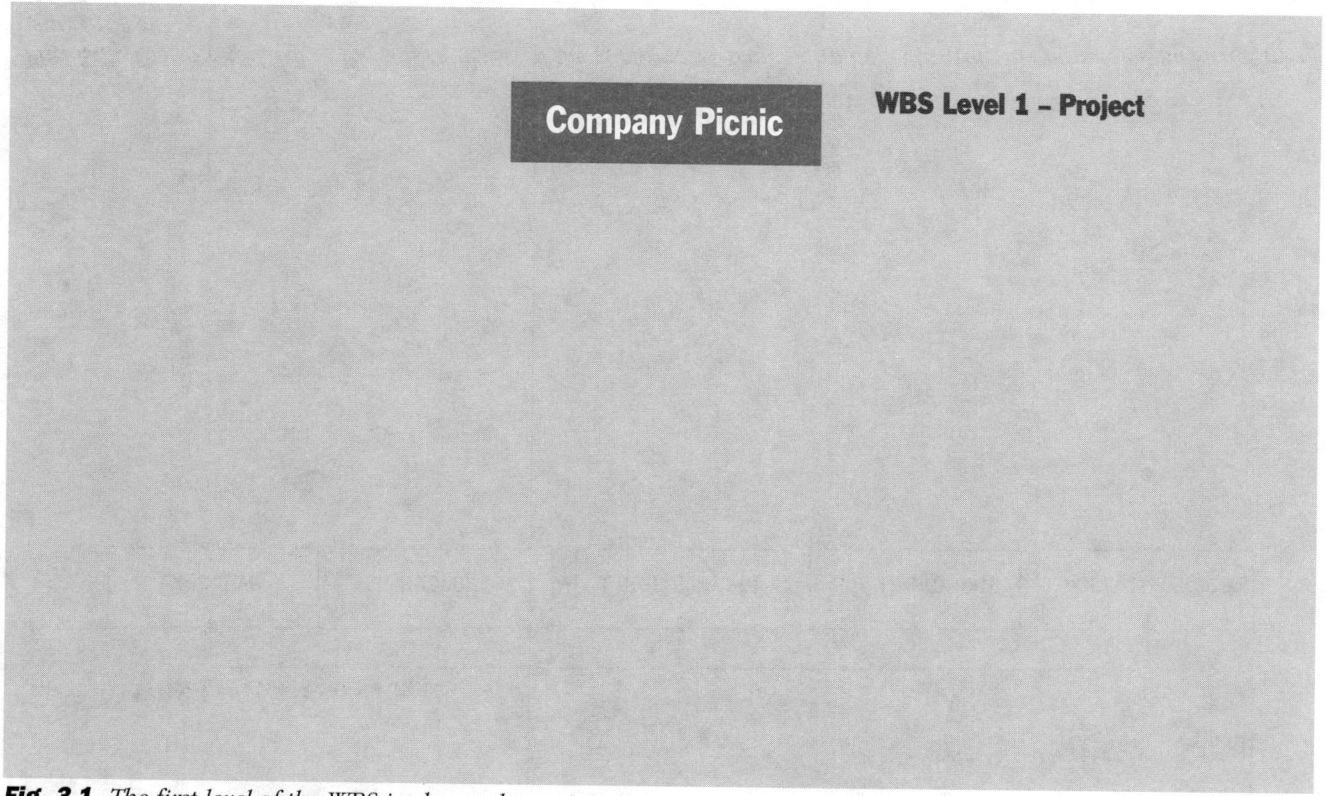

WBS Level 1 – Project

Company Picnic

Fig. 3.1. *The first level of the WBS is always the project.*

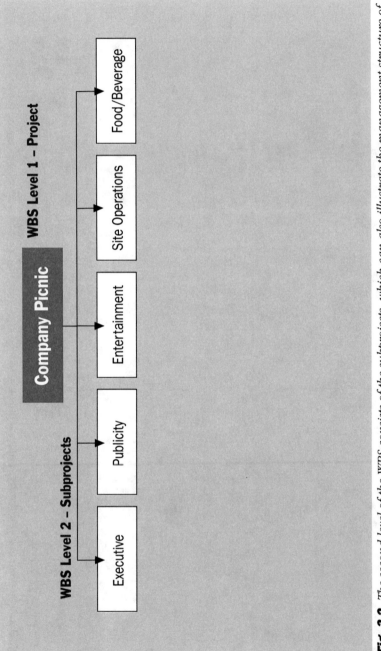

Fig. 3.2. *The second level of the WBS consists of the subprojects, which can also illustrate the management structure of your project.*

It's worth taking the time to think about your subproject structure. The subproject structure for the picnic WBS is set up by *functional* area. Other possibilities are:

- **Chronological/Phased.** The NASA moon project was set up using a roughly chronological approach to the WBS (see fig. 3.3). You can also conceive of this as grouping by phases.

- **Discipline.** Often, a building construction project will group tasks by skilled trade area (see fig 3.4).

- **Cross-departmental.** Sometimes, a project uses the existing organizational structure. If the jobs on the project will each be done by an existing department (e.g., Marketing does some tasks, Engineering others), you'll naturally use the departments as your Level 2 subprojects (see fig. 3.5).

If your WBS subproject structure helps you to understand and assign the work, you've done it right.

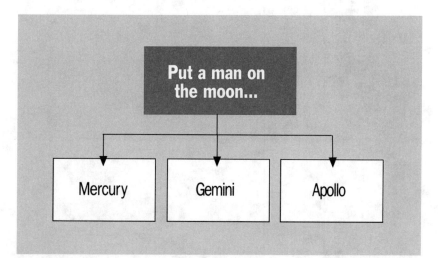

Fig. 3.3. *A WBS with a chronological/phased approach to the subproject structure.*

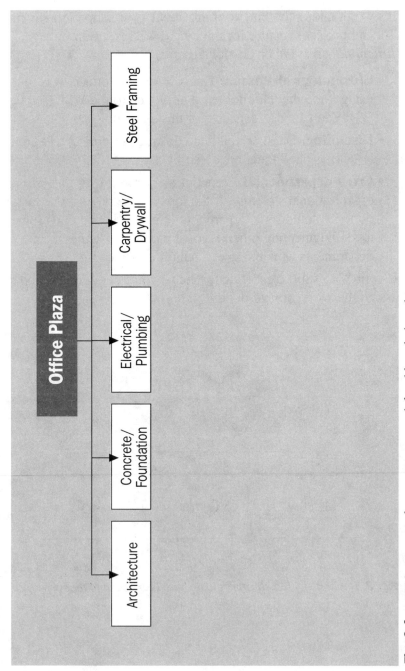

Fig. 3.4. *A WBS using a subproject structure defined by job discipline.*

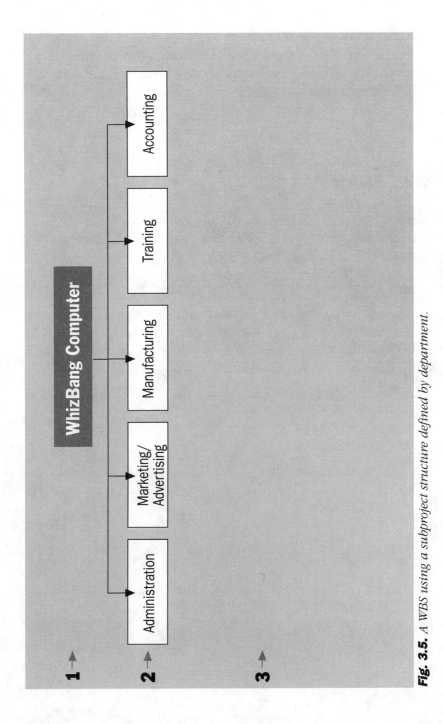

Fig. 3.5. *A WBS using a subproject structure defined by department.*

3. **Assign tasks to the WBS.** Level 3 of your WBS is the Task level (see fig. 3.6). Take the tasks and assign them to the subprojects, grouping like with like. Don't worry at this time whether your tasks are listed in the expected order of accomplishment. Sequencing of tasks comes later.

WBS Shortcut

The advantage of listing your tasks on sticky notes is that you can easily create your WBS using a whiteboard. Make a new sticky sheet for the project itself. That's Level 1. Make sheets for each subproject. (*Tip!* Use a different color for each subproject, and use the same color for the tasks that go under it. Color-coding the WBS makes it easier to track who's responsible for each task, and even what category of task it is.) Finally, group the task sticky note sheets under each subproject. You're finished!

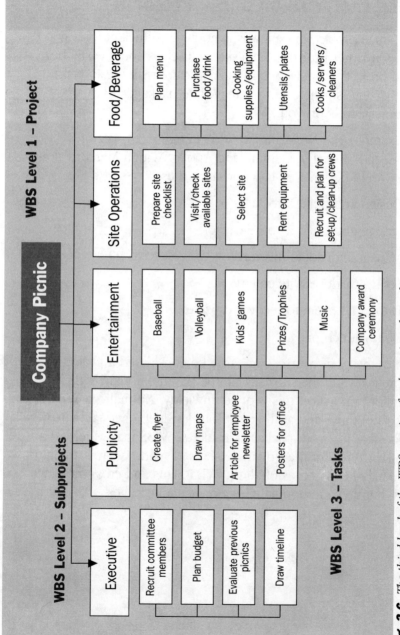

Fig. 3.6. *The third level of the WBS consist of tasks assigned to subprojects.*

Using the WBS on Large Projects

On a small project, three levels is normally sufficient for a good WBS. On larger projects, the tasks themselves could easily be called projects in their own right. You can break these "task/projects" into smaller, more manageable packages, creating additional levels on your WBS.

For example, the NASA Project WBS in figure 3.3 has three subprojects: Mercury, Gemini, and Apollo. Within Mercury alone, there would be Level 3 "tasks" such as these:

- Design and build a rocket.
- Design and build a space capsule.
- Manage individual missions.
- Set up worldwide telemetry.
- Design a system to recover capsules.
- Build launch pads.

Each of these, of course, can easily be considered a project. Theoretically, all the subtasks can be put into a giant WBS pyramid. In practice, this is quite unwieldy. Normally, a WBS consists of three and at the most four levels. Individual managers responsible for work packages inside the WBS make their own WBS structures for their own elements of work. A project control office may keep copies of all the WBS plans and cross-reference them, but they are normally kept on separate pages.

Large projects often number tasks to make controlling them easier. If you number tasks, you should number subtasks as well, since the subtasks go into the master plan.

Here is a key insight in managing large projects using a WBS. Whether you are the manager at the top of the WBS pyramid, or a "subproject" manager in the middle, two things are always true:

1. You need to know the general shape of the pyramid and what's going on.

2. You need to focus on your primary responsibility, which is that area of the pyramid under your control. When your project is part of a larger whole, your mission is to complete your project in line with that goal, not as an end in itself.

Exercise #4:

Installing a LAN System as a Sample Project

For this exercise, create a sample project and follow it through the planning process. So far, you've learned to develop a good objective and a WBS.

Project: You have been assigned to manage a project to install a local area network (LAN) in an office of twenty-five people, each of whom has an individual computer station. The LAN will consist of a single server (host computer), the wiring to connect the individual computers scattered around the office, and the software to operate the LAN. The LAN should provide the following features: e-mail, file sharing, and cost reductions (people will be able to use the same printers and peripherals). Your boss has given you a budget of $40,000 and told you the project must be completed before the start of the new fiscal year (September 30), which is 16 weeks away, to keep the budget authority.

Part 1

1. Identify the Triple Constraints.

    Project: _____

    Performance criteria: _____

    Budget constraint: _____

    Time constraint: _____

2. Rank the Triple Constraints.

    Driver: _____

    Middle constraint: _____

    Weak constraint: _____

Answers to Sample Project Triple Constraints, Part 1

1. Identify the Triple Constraints.

Project:	Install LAN
Performance criteria:	E-mail, file sharing, printer sharing
Budget constraint:	$40,000
Time constraint:	Before next fiscal year (16 weeks)

2. Rank the Triple Constraints.

Driver:	Time
Middle constraint:	Budget
Weak constraint:	Performance

In this situation, you wouldn't be completely sure about the Triple Constraint ranking without doing some more investigation. But based solely on what you know now, it would make sense to regard Time as the driver, since the expiration of your budget authority would make the project fall apart.

The $40,000 budget and the criteria for what the LAN should accomplish are less certain. In this case, the primary costs will be for hardware. You probably have more flexibility as to the features and speed of the new LAN; it will also be easier to modify the LAN later if more or better features are desired. The likely situation, therefore, is that Budget is the middle constraint and Performance is the weak constraint.

Part 2

Brainstorm and group the tasks. Use sticky notes (or simply an additional piece of paper or the blank WBS on the next page) to brainstorm the tasks necessary for this project. Create your groups and prepare a preliminary WBS using the groups as your second level and your tasks as the third level.

One version of the WBS for this LAN project is shown in figure 4.1. It will likely differ from yours; this doesn't mean your answer is wrong. Different project managers will inevitably organize the same project in a different fashion, and there's nothing wrong with that. Do compare the two versions. Does yours have reasonable subprojects? Are your tasks complete? Did you forget anything?

Now that you have experience in creating a WBS, turn to the next chapter to learn how to turn the WBS into a plan.

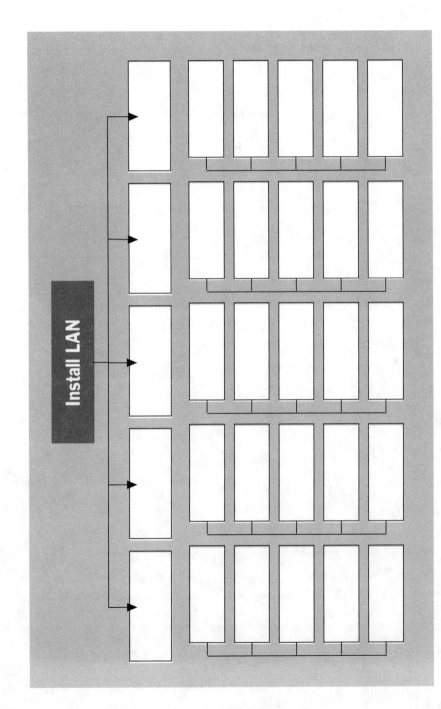

Laying Out the Project

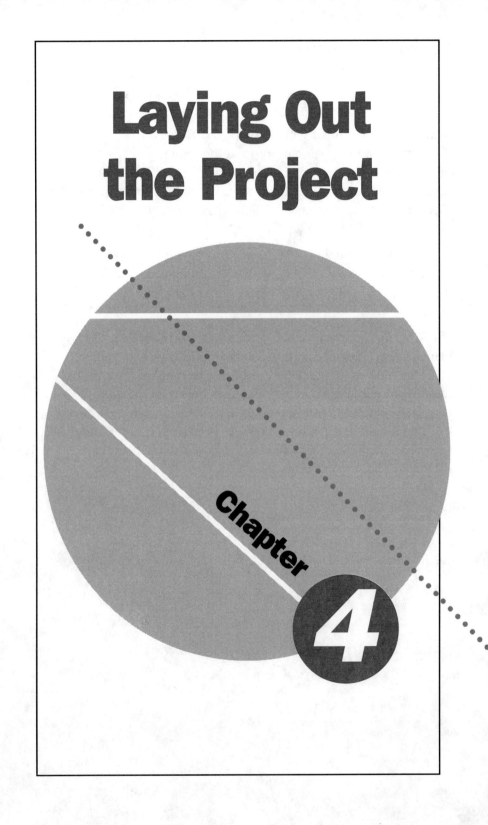

Chapter

4

Now that you're armed with a completed WBS, you're ready for the next step in the planning process: determining the sequence of activities. As you learned earlier, one of the characteristics of a project is that it can be broken into tasks that can be sequenced. How you choose your task sequence has a substantial impact on the outcome of your project.

Return to your sample LAN project. You have prepared your version of a WBS by identifying and grouping tasks. Remember, the version in figure 4.1 is not necessarily more correct than yours.

The WBS in figure 4.1 identifies four subproject areas: project management, purchasing, installation and testing, and training. The logic here is a combination of functional breakdown and rough chronological (purchasing comes before installation, installation comes before training). This does not mean, however, that the tasks in each WBS subproject will happen in the order shown on the WBS. That's the next step of project planning: creating a *Dependency Sequence*.

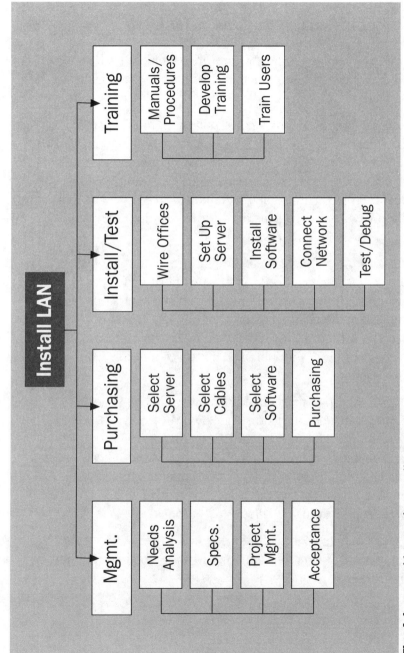

Fig. 4.1. *A possible WBS for installing a LAN.*

Project Management as a Task

Do you treat the work of project management itself as a task? Experts disagree whether it should be listed as a task in the WBS.

Here are some reasons against putting it in: Project management isn't a "task" in the manner of the actual work. Nothing is dependent on project management; that is, no task is waiting for project management to finish so that it can begin. Project management is ongoing, from the outset of the project to the conclusion. It doesn't fit into the planning and sequencing process.

Reasons for putting it in: Although it may not be a task, project management does involve work. It consumes resources. If you're a full-time project manager, your time and salary are charged against the project. If you don't account for the resource costs of project management in the WBS, you must be doubly certain to account for them elsewhere.

If you are a part-time project manager, that is, you must perform technical tasks on your own project while providing overall direction, notice that project management is consuming a portion of a resource that would otherwise be available full-time for task accomplishment. Again, you must be sure to budget out the project management resource. The WBS approach makes this nearly automatic.

Project management is listed as a task in the WBS for the sample LAN project in figure 4.1 to show the consumption of the resource.

Planning as a Task

Why isn't the activity of planning shown as a task on the WBS? Although planning is a time-consuming activity, it normally doesn't go into the WBS. After all, the WBS and other planning documents are the result of the planning process. Planning is finished when the project begins.

If you're running a project with unusually complicated and difficult planning issues, you can make planning a separate project, with the result of the project being a plan to accomplish the next project.

Creating a Dependency Sequence Using "Sticky Note PERT"

Before you can create a Dependency Sequence, you must be familiar with these terms:

A *dependent task* is a task that can't begin until one or more predecessor tasks are complete. For example, if you're planning to install a swimming pool in your back yard, you must first dig a hole—and then pour in the concrete. (Doing it backwards would obviously be ineffective.) Pouring concrete is *dependent* on digging the hole. Digging the hole is the *predecessor* task to pouring concrete. In project management language, the words *dependent* and *predecessor* are usually reserved for the specific tasks immediately before and following the subject task, even though there may be a long string of tasks before and after.

A *parallel task* is a task that may be performed during the same time frame as other tasks. For example, you could landscape the area around the swimming pool at the same time you were putting paint and sealant on the pool concrete, as these tasks do not directly interfere with each other.

A *lag task* is a task that must be shown in the work flow although it has no work associated with it. For example, when you pour the concrete for your swimming pool, the concrete must cure before you can paint and seal it. Although that takes waiting, or "lag," time, it doesn't require any work. Some project management authorities show lag tasks merely as gaps in the schedule; however, it's best to show these tasks so you won't accidentally forget them.

A *dummy task* in the planning technique known as "activity-on-arrow PERT" is an arrow that shows a dependency relationship between two otherwise parallel tasks. You'll learn about that type of dummy task in greater detail later in this book.

A *milestone task* is a task that requires no time or budget, but must be shown in the work flow. Milestones are often checkpoints, starting lines, finishing lines, or report dates. For example, a milestone in the swimming pool project could be "Start Swimming!" This task would simply mark the moment when people could dive in. There's no work or time involved, just a milestone. In a project timeline, a milestone is often shown with a diamond symbol (♦).

In Chapter 3, you were strongly encouraged to use sticky notes in different colors to create your WBS. In this chapter, you will learn how to use those colored note sheets as a valuable shortcut—one that's nicknamed "Sticky Note PERT." PERT, or "Program Evaluation and Review Technique," is a powerful and sophisticated tool for planning projects. Usually, only skilled project managers running large projects use PERT. Managers of smaller projects often avoid it because of its reputation for complexity; they use the Gantt chart technique instead.

While the Gantt chart (covered in Chapter 7) is extremely useful for small projects, you should still learn the basics of PERT project layout, no matter how small your projects are.

To create a Sticky Note PERT chart, take your Level 3 task notes from your WBS and place them in the order you think they should be performed. Draw lines or arrows between the notes. The resulting drawing is called a PERT chart.

You can gain many insights about your project by completing a PERT chart. You'll normally discover that while some tasks can only be put together in a single sequence, you often can make a *strategic choice* that has a profound impact on the ultimate outcome of your project.

Figure 4.2 shows a Sticky Note PERT chart created from the Install LAN WBS.

Here's how to use the sticky notes to create a PERT chart: Begin by taking the sheets for "Needs Analysis" and "Project Management" and making those the lead-off tasks in the project. Remember, "Project Management" isn't a task in the same sense as "Needs Analysis," since nothing is dependent on its completion.

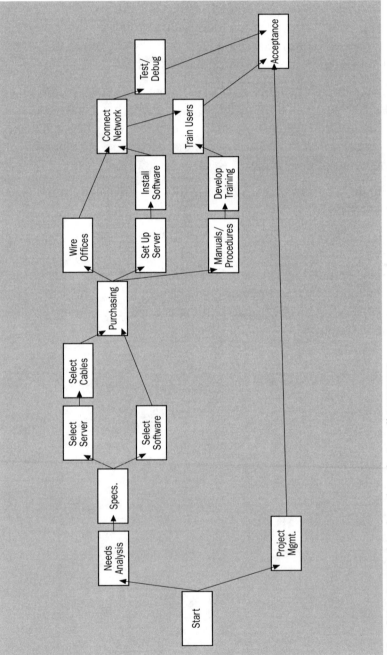

Fig. 4.2. *A PERT chart based on the Install LAN WBS.*

If your project begins or ends with more than one task going on simultaneously, it's a good idea to start with an extra "dummy" activity so that all the lines come together at both ends of the project. The "Start" box in figure 4.2 is an example. You don't need a "Finish" box in this example because all lines connect up in the final "Acceptance" box.

Once the "Needs Analysis" is complete, you can develop project specifications, so "Specs" is one item that follows "Needs Analysis" in the chart. So far, most project managers would lay out this project in the exact same way. However, the next step isn't so straightforward and clear.

When you have an option in laying out project tasks, first list all the possibilities and analyze their pros and cons. Then and only then, make your strategic decision. As you continue with your planning process, you may uncover additional information to support or conflict with your previous decision. Revisit your layout decision as necessary until you've made the best choices for your project.

Making the Strategic Choice

You know you must shop before you buy, and the LAN project requires you to shop for three items: the server (a computer that will run the LAN), the cables and connectors that will bring all the computers together into the network, and the software package that will run the LAN. As you plan, notice that you can do the shopping in several different orders. You may already have an idea of the smart way to do this, but before you make a decision, always list the possibilities. Figure 4.3 provides four options for doing so.

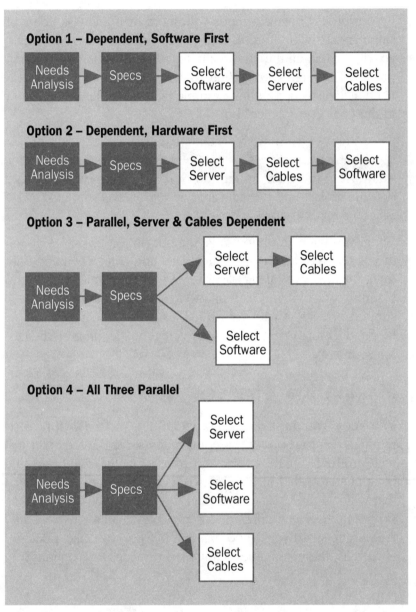

Fig. 4.3. *Four options for shopping for LAN equipment. When you have more than one option for when to perform a project task, you have a strategic choice.*

Option 1 is to lay the tasks out in a straight dependency sequence and to select software first, followed by the server and then the cables. Since the software package determines the ultimate functions of the LAN, you can make a strong case for choosing this method: You'll necessarily put your emphasis on choosing the perfect software first and then buying hardware and cables to meet your software needs.

Option 2 simply reverses the selection process: You'll choose the hardware elements first, and then the software. Because you already have an installed base of computers, you might need to ensure hardware compatibility. Or, you may have special discount purchasing arrangements with certain vendors, and those vendors have a limited selection. Or, since the hardware costs more than the software, budget limitations might force you to pick the server and cables first, and then to narrow your software search to what will run on what you can afford to buy.

Option 3 puts the hardware tasks on one parallel track and the software tasks on another. How can you do this? Assuming that you have done a good job analyzing the needs and developing the specifications, you have enough information to assign the shopping to two different people and send them out. *The key advantage of this method is saving time.* But what is the cost of saving time (you know you can't get something for nothing)? The price of saving time is additional resources—putting another person on the task. Notice that one person (assuming proper skills) can do all the work in either Option 1 or Option 2, but it will take more time. In Option 3, two people can go to different stores simultaneously, reducing calendar time but increasing resources. Time versus resource tradeoffs is a critical tool you will use to achieve project goals.

If some parallel tasking is good, would more be better? Option 4 points out that you could send three people shopping and get server, cables, and software at the same time. Again, this assumes that specifications are well-drawn and complete.

None of these options is right and the others wrong. Any one of these options might be the right one for your project circumstances. The point is this: Only when you list and study the options do you have the power to pick the best one for your project.

For the sake of this example, Option 3 was chosen. Why? First, the Time constraint has been established as the driver. Parallel tasks save time. Why not Option 4, then? Here's one rationale: Selecting the cables before selecting the server is risky, so the small amount of time parallel tasking would save wouldn't be worth it. Notice that this is just one opinion. Yours need not be the same—when you're the project manager.

To finish your project layout, you'll make similar decisions throughout the network. Here's the logic behind some of the decisions for the PERT chart shown in figure 4.2.

1. To "Train Users," you need "Develop Training" and "Connect Network" to be complete. Arguably, you could do the training off site at the vendor's location, using the vendor's LAN. This is a quality versus time trade-off decision.

2. "Test/Debug" will need to be done in two phases. The first phase will consist of the testing that must be completed to allow the "Train Users" task to begin. The second phase consists of additional work that can parallel and follow "Train Users." This phase will include issues the users themselves identify, plus minor problems that can be fixed at any time. We have a choice of breaking "Test/Debug" into two separate tasks, or of setting up the schedule so the tasks overlap.

3. "Project Management" actually ends after the "Acceptance" phase is over. Sometimes, a milestone (♦) for "End of Project" is placed in the plan so that "Project Management" will have something to connect to.

Risk and Resource Management in Dependency Sequencing

You've learned that one important issue in choosing task sequence options is time. Two others are *risk* and *resources*.

Risk Management

Some tasks are inherently riskier than others. Risk means likelihood of task failure, which can come in any of the Triple Constraints: a task can be late, over budget, or fail to achieve its performance requirements.

The placement of a task in the dependency sequence can increase or decrease risk. One argument against choosing Option 3 for hardware/software selection (see figs. 4.2 and 4.3) is that it's riskier to have two people off choosing hardware and software than for one person to do it in a dependent sequence. Making the tasks parallel arguably increases risk. This doesn't mean that you shouldn't sequence the tasks in this way, but you should at least be aware of the risk.

Sometimes, paralleling tasks can lower risk. Let's assume that selecting the hardware and cables together will take less time than selecting the software. *Parallel tasks need not take exactly the same amount of time to complete.* Since the start of "Purchasing" requires that all the selection work has been completed, you have extra time available to select hardware and cables, measured by:

$$Time_{(Software)} - (Time_{(Server)} + Time_{(Cables)}) = Time_{(Slack)}$$

Slack time is the extra time available to complete the shorter parallel tasks. It's another "hidden resource" for the professional project manager. You'll learn much more about slack time in later chapters. For now, remember this key point: *slack lowers risk.* When there's extra time before the successor task begins, lateness in a task (as long as it doesn't exceed the available slack) isn't critical. Given extra time, you may be able to improve conformance to performance standards or even control costs. While slack doesn't eliminate risk altogether, many problems can be solved with a little extra time.

You may discover additional risk issues on your tasks as you continue the planning process. If necessary, revisit the dependency sequence and, where possible, replan to put high-risk tasks where slack is available.

Resource Management

Choosing to shop for software parallel to shopping for the server and cables presupposes that you have the staff available to do both jobs simultaneously. In reality, you may not. Since making tasks parallel saves time at the expense of resources, you must have the resources available in the first place.

For example, if you've set up all your tasks so that they are "full-time equivalent" (i.e., every task takes a full-time person for its duration), and you have three people on your project team, you can't make more than three tasks parallel at any one time.

You may have a situation in which a dependency relationship exists between two tasks, not because the tasks are related, but because the second task can't begin until the person performing the first task finishes with that task. *Resources, then, can force dependency relationships.*

When you manage multiple, simultaneous projects, you may have cross-project dependencies. If the same team handles multiple projects, Worker A may do Task A for Project B and then move on to do Task D for Project C. If Worker A runs overschedule on Task A, Task D necessarily starts late. Therefore, in a very real sense, Task D/Project C is dependent on Task A/Project B—a cross-project dependency.

Managing these complex work and resource relationships is one of the chief benefits of planning. Only by identifying all the potential conflicts can you hope to resolve them.

Types of Dependencies

The common understanding of "dependency" is that if Task B is dependent upon Task A, then Task B can't start until Task A is complete. This is called a *finish-to-start (FS) dependency.* While it's the most frequently-encountered type of dependency, it's not the only one. As you lay out your project, you'll encounter various types of dependencies, including these:

- Finish-to-finish (FF) dependency
- Start-to-start (SS) dependency
- Start-to-finish (SF) dependency
- Overlaps
- Lag

The rest of this chapter focuses on each of these dependencies.

Finish-to-Finish (FF) Dependency

The finish of Task B is dependent upon the finish of Task A in a finish-to-finish dependency. Task B can begin before or during Task A, but it needs the finish of Task A before it can conclude.

For example, "Connect Network" is currently FS dependent on "Wire Offices." (See fig. 4.2.) You will wire all the offices, and when you're finished, you'll connect the computers.

Instead, you could make "Connect Network" FF dependent on "Wire Offices": You connect the individual computers as you wire each office. However, the absolute final stages of "Connect Network" require "Wire Offices" to be complete.

Like parallel tasking, an FF dependency can save time and may also improve the efficiency of the work.

Start-to-Start (SS) Dependency

In a start-to-start dependency, the start of Task B is dependent upon the start of Task A. You could make "Manuals/Procedures" SS dependent upon "Purchasing."

Instead of starting the manuals and procedures as soon as you've made the hardware and software choices, you might wait until the beginning of purchasing, especially if you anticipate, for example, that it might be difficult to buy the hardware and software you selected. As soon as "Purchasing" begins, making the selections official, you can start on "Manuals/Procedures."

Start-to-Finish (SF) Dependency

A seldom-used relationship, a start-to-finish dependency indicates that the finish of Task B depends on the start of Task A.

You might decide to make "Set up Server" SF-dependent on "Wire Offices" because you can't finish "Set Up Server" until at least one office has been wired.

Overlaps

Sometimes there is a relationship between tasks that doesn't involve the exact start or finish. You can overlap these tasks. For example, in figure 4.2, "Purchasing" may be FS-dependent upon "Select Cables" and "Select Software" for efficiency reasons. (Some organizations have complex procurement processes, and doing it all together may be desirable.) But, on the other hand, you might be able to use an overlap relationship for these tasks. Start the purchasing process after the starts of "Select Server" and "Select Software," buying each item in the mix as soon as the selection decision is made. By overlapping the tasks, "Purchasing" finishes ahead of when it might have if you had waited until all the selection decisions were made.

Overlap can be described in time, task, or percentage terms:

- Start "Purchasing" one week after the beginning of the selection tasks. (Time)

- Start "Purchasing" as soon as the first selection item is completed. (Task)

- Start "Purchasing" with a 25 percent overlap on "Select Server." (Percentage—this means that "Purchasing" begins after 25 percent of "Select Server" is complete.)

Lag

Imagine that you purchased your server, cables, and software by mail order. Now you have a lag between the time when the purchase is complete and the time when you can begin "Wire Office" and "Set Up Server." That time lag is the time you spend waiting for the packages to arrive. It's easy to forget lag when you're mapping out a project plan—make sure you account for any delays.

Tip: For significant periods of "lag," draw it in the project schedule so you can't forget it.

Remember, at this point, you should consider your project layout tentative. You need a basic layout so you can continue the process. By creating a basic layout, you've made some strategic decisions, but you still don't have all the facts. Revisit the project layout as you gain greater knowledge of your project, since decisions about your final layout have a substantial impact on your project's outcome.

Exercise #5:

Making Your Own "Sticky Note PERT"

You've been asked to put together a word processing system for your department secretary. The system is to consist of a computer, a word processing package, and a printer. Using the WBS shown below, create a Sticky Note PERT layout. For the purposes of this exercise, try to make tasks parallel when possible. Assume all dependencies are FS-type.

You will need some sticky notes or small sheets of paper and a surface to lay them out on.

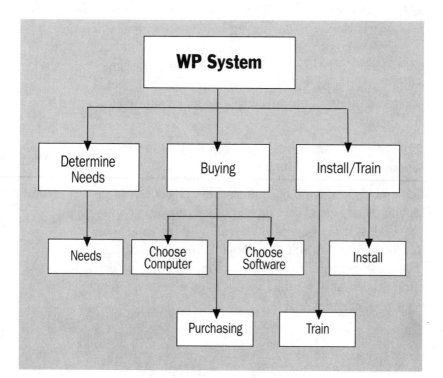

Answer to Exercise #5

Here is one possible project layout. If you've made different choices, you haven't necessarily completed the exercise incorrectly. Compare this version to your own version to check your understanding of the process.

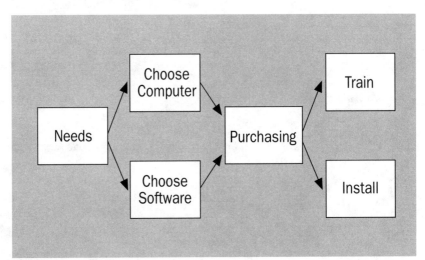

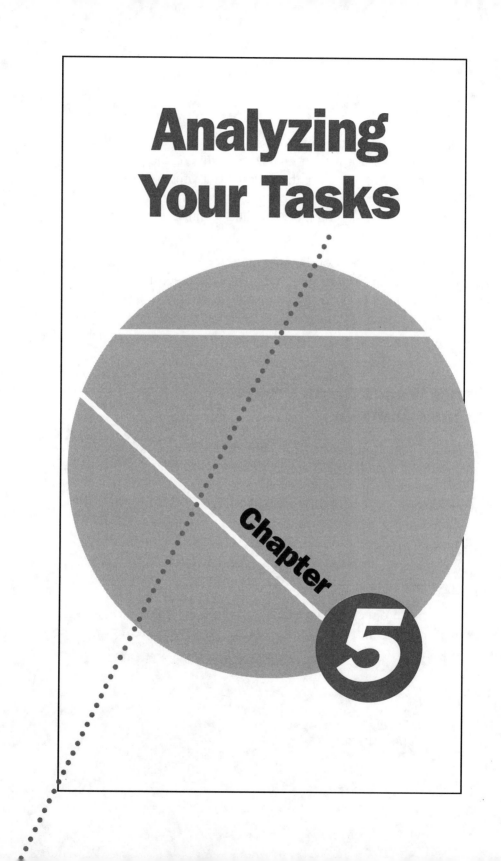

Analyzing Your Tasks

Chapter 5

Part of properly understanding your project is understanding the details of the tasks that make it up. *Task analysis* is the process of studying your tasks, gathering the various data you need to manage the tasks, writing specifications, constructing estimates for task performance, assigning the work, and identifying potential problems.

As with any other aspect of the planning process, take your time and do the task analysis process right. Drawing together in a single place all the information you need allows you to give better and clearer work assignments, to look realistically at management issues, and to control the performance of the actual work.

Large Versus Small Projects in Task Analysis

Different types of projects require different levels of task analysis detail. Complex projects, especially those involving large dollar-value contracts, require highly detailed specifications, sometimes running into hundreds of pages. Smaller projects may benefit from shorter, less detailed specifications that rely more on the initiative and judgment of the person responsible for each task.

How detailed does your task analysis need to be? To answer that question, think about the following issues:

1. How much direct management control will you have over the work to be performed? (More control = less need to document in advance)

Sequence First or Task First?

Should you plan the sequence first or analyze the tasks first? Project management authorities disagree.

Planning the sequence first gives you the advantage of analyzing your tasks in their proper context. Tasks are affected by their predecessors, and they affect their successors.

On the other hand, by analyzing the tasks first, you gain more detailed task knowledge. This information can be useful as you make decisions about risk and resource issues that are inherent in parallel tasking. You may be able to construct a better dependency sequence as a result.

Although this book plans sequence first and analyzes tasks second, there is actually third—and better—option: Integrate the two steps. Gather easily available task data and prepare a rough dependency sequence. Add detailed task analysis information, and then revisit the dependency sequence. Work back and forth until you've refined your project plan. In the real world, planning seldom fits the one-step-at-a-time model shown in workbooks.

Planning is an iterative process. The knowledge you gain as you work through each step often forces you to redo earlier steps in the process.

2. What level of confidence do you have in the capability and positive motivation of your detail team to achieve the goal? (More capability/better motivation = less need for detail)

3. What are the consequences of a significant misunderstanding? (Minor consequences = less need for detail)

Specifications can't be made fool-proof, as the sage said, because fools are so ingenious. Highly detailed contract specifications exist primarily to deal with payment issues. If you need them, do them—but if you don't, don't.

A Form for Task Analysis

The sample form in figure 5.1 shows the information you need to gather for each project task. You may use this form or create your own version. Don't feel restricted by the size of the form, or feel obligated to fill it up; the amount of information you need necessarily varies by the type of project and project conditions.

You must, however, answer these questions:

- Who's going to do each task?

- How long will each task take?

- How much will the task cost?

- What are the deliverables/outcomes of the task?

Task Analysis Form
Task No.:
Task Name:
Predecessor Task(s):
Successor Task(s):
Specifications/Deliverables: • _____ • _____
Resources—People/Department: • _____ • _____
Equipment/Supplies: • _____ • _____
Time Estimate: "Must Start" _____ "Must Finish" _____
Milestones: • _____ • _____ Optimistic _____ Pessimistic _____ Most Likely _____

Cost Estimate:
    Salaries $_____
    Equipment/Supplies $_____
    Contract Costs $_____
    Overhead @ ____% $_____
    TOTAL $_____

Fig. 5.1. *The success of any project depends on how well you analyze each individual task. A Task Analysis Form similar to the one shown here can aid you in analyzing a project's tasks.*

Completing a Task Analysis

Let's take a task from the LAN project and complete a task analysis form for it. Let's choose the task "Wire Offices."

This task involves stringing wire through ceiling panels and walls to reach twenty-five individual computer stations.

Task Number

You'll find it convenient to number your tasks. You can number tasks sequentially (1 to X), or you can create your own system. For the LAN project, the elements of the WBS are numbered first as follows:

1. Management

2. Purchasing

3. Install/Test

4. Training

"Wire Offices" is the first task in the third WBS category, making it Task 3-1 (see fig. 5.2).

Task Name

The Task Name in this example is obviously "Wire Offices." You can simply use the name you gave the task in the third level of the WBS.

Task No:	Task Name:
3-1	Wire Offices

Fig. 5.2. *The Task Analysis Form provides a place to record the Task number and the Task name.*

Predecessor and Successor Tasks

Using the Dependency Sequence, you can identify the tasks that come before (predecessor tasks) and after (successor tasks) the subject task (current task). Notice in figure 5.3 that "Purchasing" is the fourth task in the second WBS category and "Connect Network" is the fourth task in the third WBS category.

Predecessor Task(s)	Successor Task(s)
2-4 Purchasing	3-4 Connect Network

Fig. 5.3. *The predecessor task comes before the current task; the successor task comes after. It's important to note these on the Task Analysis Form.*

Specifications and Deliverables

Specifications are the detailed performance criteria the task must achieve. *Deliverables* are the end products the task must achieve. You may list either or both on the Task Analysis Form, depending on your project.

While detailed specifications and deliverables may go on for page after page, you should identify particularly vital requirements up front. For example, the requirement that the wiring must not disrupt departmental work (see fig. 5.4) is more important than other details, such as outlet boxes must be within 6 inches of the wall baseboards.

Specifications/Deliverables:

- Cable must connect all 25 workstations to central server.
- Wire to be completely encased in wall or ceiling.
- Must avoid disrupting department work.

Fig. 5.4. *Use the Task Analysis Form to note the vital specifications and deliverables.*

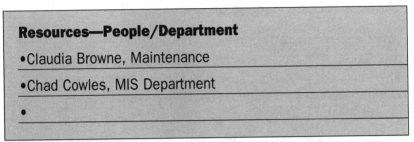

> **Resources—People/Department**
>
> • Claudia Browne, Maintenance
>
> • Chad Cowles, MIS Department
>
> •

Fig. 5.5. *Assigning people to the tasks requires thoughtful analysis. If you don't have enough information at this point to assign actual people, list the skills team members will need to complete the tasks.*

Human Resources

Allocating human resources to tasks is one of the most complex parts of task analysis. You must take into account the following:

- **Skills.** Can the people you have available to you do the job?
- **Availability.** Can the people you are considering be there when you need them?
- **Other obligations.** What other responsibilities and commitments do these people have? These impact availability.

You may find that you don't have enough information to properly allocate resources to tasks at this stage of the planning process. Instead of assigning people, assign skills. For example, instead of "Claudia," you could write: "60 people-hours of work requiring skills in wiring and building maintenance. Assign team consisting of maintenance and MIS people." As the planning process continues, you can choose the actual team members (see fig. 5.5).

Equipment/Supplies

Forcing yourself to think about the supplies and equipment can help avoid costly surprises later. Be sure to consider every aspect of the task. Recall from Chapter 2 how easy it was to forget such essential items as utensils and paper plates when planning for the company picnic. Don't overlook the obvious! (See fig. 5.6.)

Equipment/Supplies

- Stepladder, wire fish equipment, cable, outlet boxes, standard toolbox.
- All tools available in-office except for cable and outlet boxes.

Fig. 5.6. *Notice that in addition to listing the tools needed, it's a good idea to note where they can be obtained.*

Time and Cost

So far in the task analysis you've dealt with information that is fixed and definite, or at least that you can make fixed and definite. Time and cost issues are more difficult to analyze because they require you to predict the future and make plans based on the unknown. You have to make estimates, and you are held responsible for the quality of those estimates.

Throughout your project management career, you'll regularly be asked to predict the unpredictable. Use the techniques in the accompanying chart to hone your estimating skills.

Six Tips to Exceptional Estimating

1. Use actual time estimates from similar tasks in other projects. Good estimates are based on historical data; use the best historical data you can find.

2. Involve the person most knowledgeable about the task and ask for his or her estimates. But be sure to learn that person's tendencies: Are you dealing with someone who is an optimist—or a pessimist? (Some people claim to be realists. They're usually pessimists.)

3. Research the history of the vendors and subcontractors you plan to use. How experienced are they? How reliable have their estimates been in the past? Get references and check them out.

4. Look for standard reference books containing time estimates. From the standard garage book that says how long it should take a mechanic to fix your car to software industry norms for the development of code, many references exist for specific work-types. Check your trade or professional organization for details.

5. Be especially cautious when estimating for tasks whose outcome and timing directly affect the final project outcome. When possible, build in extra time and resources to allow "slack" for those tasks.

6. Train yourself to be an exceptional estimator. Whenever you need an estimate, make an "off-the-top-of-your-head" guess and write it down. Then make an estimate. When you finish the actual work, compare the actual result to your guess. By giving your brain regular feedback, you'll find yourself becoming progressively more accurate.

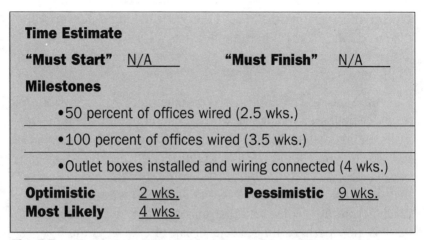

Time Estimate

"Must Start"   N/A   **"Must Finish"**   N/A

Milestones

• 50 percent of offices wired (2.5 wks.)

• 100 percent of offices wired (3.5 wks.)

• Outlet boxes installed and wiring connected (4 wks.)

| **Optimistic** | 2 wks. | **Pessimistic** | 9 wks. |
| **Most Likely** | 4 wks. | | |

Fig. 5.7. *Estimating the time required to complete a task isn't an exact science, but you can learn to make fairly accurate estimates. Record them on the Task Analysis Form.*

"Must Start"/"Must Finish" dates. Most tasks have an "as soon as possible" start condition; that is, they start at the earliest moment their predecessor tasks allow. Occasionally, a task may be more restricted. For example, if the wiring of your offices was being done in a new building and you had contracted with a drywall crew to come in on a certain date to put up the interior walls, then you might assign a "Must Finish" date to "Wire Offices."

In general, Must Start/Must Finish dates should be used only when necessary (see fig. 5.7).

Milestones. Milestones are checkpoints that are built into projects so you can monitor actual progress. As you can see in figure 5.7, the first wiring parts are expected to take longer than the later ones because of a learning curve. A 50 percent wiring completion milestone is set as the first checkpoint. The second checkpoint comes when all the basic wiring is done. The final phase of the work is connecting up the wiring. The final checkpoint is also the end of the task.

Optimistic/Pessimistic/Most Likely. How long will it actually take to do the work? When the task has a relatively low risk, assign the Most Likely time based on your estimating; then go on to the next section.

Sometimes tasks have high risk. For example, if you're working in an older building, you won't know about conditions behind the walls until you start drilling. If you're lucky and the space is easy to work in, you should be able to finish relatively quickly, say in two weeks. That's the *optimistic* outcome. But there's a chance that the walls, as constructed, won't allow the wiring to take place according to plan and that major work will be necessary to get it done—perhaps nine weeks. That, of course, is the *pessimistic* outcome. However, if the building is like others of similar vintage, which is *most likely*, you'll encounter some minor problems but should be able to get the job done in four weeks (see fig. 5.7).

Optimistic, pessimistic, and most likely values are used in PERT time estimating, which is discussed in Chapter 6.

Cost Estimate	
Salaries	$ _____
Equipment/Supplies	$ _____
Contract Costs	$ _____
Overhead @ ___%	$ _____
TOTAL	$ _____

Fig. 5.8. *Project costs can include fixed costs and variable costs. Salaries are a variable cost, while equipment and supplies are a fixed cost.*

For all your projects, as you've done in this example, *always estimate time first, then money.* Tasks normally have fixed costs and variable costs (see fig. 5.8). *Fixed costs* are costs for equipment and supplies. Five hundred feet of cable, far more than you need, comes on a single roll for $250. That's a fixed cost. Whether it takes two weeks, four weeks, or nine weeks to physically wire the office has a tremendous impact on the salaries portion of the task budget. That's a *variable cost.* The roll of wire costs a fixed amount regardless of installation time, but the same is not true of salaries.

Contract costs may be fixed or variable, depending on the nature of the contract. A "firm fixed price" (FFP) contract has an exact money figure attached, and is a fixed cost; a "cost plus" (CP) contract, which allows for the contractor to recover actual costs plus a percentage for gross profit, is a variable cost.

Don't forget overhead charges that may apply to your project costs. Overhead can include general and administrative (G&A) costs, salary overhead, profit margin, and other costs. They are often structured as a percentage addition to actual costs. If they will be charged to your project, then you have less real money to spend than you might have thought at first glance.

Task Analysis Time Savers

1. Although you need a Task Analysis Form for each task in your project, you don't have to prepare them all personally. Assign forms to the team members most likely to perform the work. However, do budget time to review what they produce.

2. On a large project with subtasks, prepare the forms for your Level 3 WBS tasks and assign group and team leaders to prepare forms for the deeper levels.

3. Save your Task Analysis Forms! You may be in charge of similar projects in the future that allow you to reuse (with slight edits) the forms you've already prepared.

4. If you're planning for a number of similar projects that follow a basic sequence (although each one will have unique characteristics), it's worth it to go into substantial depth on a single example and then photocopy the Task Analysis sheets for all the projects.

Solve Problems Easily by Catching Them Early

The Godzilla Principle says that problems grow with neglect, moving along the spectrum from easy to impossible. The technique of What If? Analysis allows you to create a Control Point Identification Chart (see fig. 5.9), a powerful tool for improving your project oversight.

In the Control Point Identification Chart, you identify something that might go wrong—or right—that would be out of the ordinary. Use a brainstorming session for each task to identify potential problems and opportunities. Then, identify early warning points and list possible solutions and strategies.

Most people plan only for things that can go wrong. This wastes another hidden resource: good luck. When things do go wrong, you must deal with them. But if you don't exploit the things that go right when they occur, you can't take advantage of their benefits.

There are three points where you may have the power to solve or eliminate a problem:

1. **When you first think of it.** If you think it might rain on your picnic, you can rent a tent or schedule a make-up date. Problem solved.

2. **At the early warning point.** In the LAN wiring example, the first wall would be the early warning point that the wall construction may be troublesome. As soon as you drill into that first wall, you'll know.

Control Point Identification Chart

Task	What could go right/wrong?	How/when would I know?	What could I do?
3-1 Wire Offices	Interior braces in walls could make wiring far more difficult and time-consuming	Early warning point: first wall	• Perhaps drill one sample wall to see if this is a problem • Provide management with early warning, as this condition would make lateness unavoidable • Draft additional help to speed up this task

Fig. 5.9. *A Control Point Identification Chart can help you anticipate problems early on and solve them before they're beyond your control.*

3. **When it happens.** Although the general strategy is to solve it early, some problems are costly or difficult to fix, or hard to predict in advance. You should still list these problems and solutions on the Control Point Identification Chart, but you don't need to act unless the problem occurs.

The chart on page 99 lists some routine problems and their possible solutions.

Showstoppers—Or, What If Godzilla Does Get to Tokyo?

If it rains on your picnic, you're responsible because you *can* plan for rain. But what if there's an earthquake? Godzilla has entered Tokyo, but this is different.

An earthquake isn't simply a problem, it's a *showstopper.* The planning process doesn't have an answer for you. Even if you had thought, "Gee, what if there's an earthquake?" it wouldn't have helped. Likewise, if you'd asked yourself "What if a nuclear bomb drops on my picnic?" or "What if aliens from outer space attack during the picnic?" you couldn't have arrived at a solution.

Obviously, this line of thinking can get ridiculous in a hurry. But the point is this: Rain is your responsibility because you can plan for it; these other catastrophes are what lawyers call Acts of God. You can't afford to worry about them, since there's nothing you can do about them if they do happen.

If you could have done something about it, it's your responsibility. If you couldn't have done anything about it, no matter how much pre-planning you might have done, then it's a showstopper.

There is one caveat you should keep in mind: if you know about a possible showstopper that could destroy the project, tell your project originators of the possibility early. For example, "Sorry, but the walls are solid concrete. It's physically impossible to run wire through them. We'll have to take a completely different approach. Here's a new set of time and budget estimates."

Common Problems and Possible Solutions	
Problem Areas	**Possible Solution**
Human Resources	• Identify replacements for each key team member. • Cross-train for critical skills.
Equipment/Facilities	• Negotiate commitments for key equipment and facilities in advance.
Capital Expenditures	• Make sure you know your organization's budget cycle and capital expenditure procedures.
Costs	• Eliminate nonessential elements. • Substitute less costly resources. • Offer a bonus for improved cost or delivery.
Administrative Procedures	• Develop detailed operating procedures and standards. • Treat support activities as "internal customers": learn their procedures and make friends.
Contracting	• Study contract issues to prepare for negotiations. • Demand compliance. • Seek alternative sources to increase your options.
Schedule Slippage	• Recover during later steps. • Narrow the scope of the work. • Throw more resources at it. • Shift resources from less time-sensitive tasks. • Contract out.

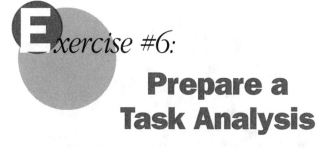

Exercise #6:

Prepare a Task Analysis

A. In the previous chapter, you put together a Sticky Note PERT chart for a word processing system. Now, prepare a mini-task analysis for one of the tasks on that PERT Chart. You'll notice that some elements on the Task Analysis Form have been eliminated because they aren't necessary on a project of this size.

Task No:
Task Name:
Predecessor Task(s):
Successor Task(s):
Specifications/Deliverables: • _____ • _____
Resources—People/Department: • _____ • _____
Equipment/Supplies: • _____ • _____

Since this is a sample project and you don't know the names of specific people, describe skills in the Resources section.

B. Answer the questions from the Control Point
Identification Chart:

   1. What could go right/wrong?

     _____

     _____

     _____

     _____

   2. How/when would I know?

     _____

     _____

     _____

     _____

   3. What could I do?

     _____

     _____

     _____

     _____

Managing Time and Cost

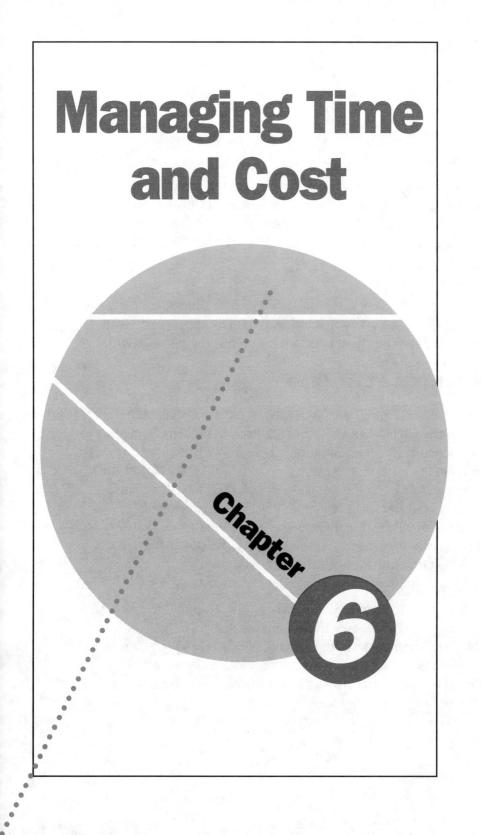

Chapter

6

"How long will it take?"

"How much will it cost?"

These two questions often strike fear into the hearts of project managers. No matter how committed they are to quality, no matter how hard they try, project managers find it difficult to predict the future. Without a crystal ball to predict the future, project managers must rely on statistical tools and techniques to get their estimates straight.

There are two fundamental approaches to time estimating: PERT and CPM (leaving aside WAG and SWAG). This chapter will focus on how you can use these two tools to predict the unpredictable.

How to Use PERT Time

During the 1950s, the United States Navy project-managed the Polaris project. This project, to build a nuclear submarine and sea-launched ICBM, was one of the most complex engineering projects in the history of the world up to that time. As part of the management process, the Navy developed PERT, the **P**rogram **E**valuation and **R**eview **T**echnique. PERT is a "soup to nuts" comprehensive project management system aimed at highly complex projects. Chapter 5 explored the task sequencing aspect of PERT, in the form we nicknamed "Sticky Note" PERT. Now, you'll learn how to estimate using the PERT technique.

The PERT time technique is used when there is high uncertainty about how long it will take to perform a given task. By using tools of statistical analysis, the PERT method allows you to create a time estimate that accounts for "good luck" and "bad luck" variables as well as to calculate the *confidence level,* which is the likelihood you'll achieve the estimated time.

Imagine that you approach an engineer on the Polaris project who designs missile guidance systems. You say: "I need a guidance system for the new ICBM that will allow us to shoot the missile from under water anywhere in the world, and then travel 3,000 miles to its destination and land within 100 yards of its target. Nothing like this has ever been done before. So, how long will it take you?"

Of course, the engineer looks at you as if you've gone crazy. "How should I know? It's R&D! If I knew in the first place, I wouldn't have to do it!"

Nevertheless, you need an answer. The duration of the system design affects the total project time constraint, the budget constraint (staff salaries), as well as numerous dependencies and other scheduled events. How can you get a meaningful answer when you understand the difficulties and uncertainties in making the estimate?

"What factors make the estimate difficult?" you might ask the engineer.

The engineer is likely to reply: "The most important factor right now is that I can think of maybe ten theoretical approaches I can take toward the design of the guidance system. I'll do my best to rank the design approaches by likelihood, but the simple truth is that I just don't know which one is the right one—at least not yet. If I get lucky, the first approach I pick might be the right one. If I'm unlucky, it might not happen until the tenth. My best guess would be the third or fourth try, which is about average for me, but I don't want to be held to that, since there's just too much uncertainty. That's why I just can't give you an answer."

Actually, the engineer's response reflects the PERT system for time estimating uncertainty. He's outlined these three possible scenarios:

T(o) = The **O**ptimistic time, or the best case with a probability of at least 1 percent.

T(p) = The **P**essimistic time, or the worst case with a probability of at least 1 percent.

T(m) = The **M**ost likely time.

Using this information, you can determine:

T(e) = The PERT **E**stimate

Returning to the Polaris project example, imagine asking the engineer:

"If you did get lucky, and the very first approach you picked turned out to be right, how long would it take you?"

The engineer's likely reply?

"About three months, but you can't put that down in your time estimate—it's not very probable."

To which you respond:

"What's the worst-case scenario?"

Engineer:

"The tenth approach does it. That makes it take about thirty months. I feel pretty safe with a thirty-month estimate."

You:

"I'll bet you do. How about the most likely case?"

Engineer:

"Well, probably nine or ten months. Say ten. That's third approach or maybe fourth. That's the most probable, but as I said, I really can't guarantee that estimate, because I just don't have the facts."

Determining the Three Estimates

How do you create the three estimates—T(o), T(p), and T(m)—given all sorts of extremes? Here are some ideas:

Historical data. Let's say your project is a grant proposal. One task is writing professional biographies of the grant staff. The staff varies by project, and the emphasis on the resumés also varies. If you have written numerous grant proposals before, calculate the fastest you've ever performed the biography stage, then the slowest, and then calculate the median.

Research. Many construction projects shut down when it rains; therefore, the amount of rain influences the number of calendar days it takes to perform a task. Historical weather data can tell you the driest and wettest months on record and provide a prediction for whether the current month is expected to be wetter or drier than average.

Published data. When you take your car to the shop, the estimated labor time (and thus the cost) for your repair are taken from standard volumes that list how long a mechanic will take to do a particular repair. Those estimates were probably created using the T(e) method; some even show ranges. Such volumes exist for many fields, including software development.

Scenarios. The engineer in the Polaris example gives three values that are scenario-based. Assuming the first approach is right is a scenario; so is assuming the last approach is the one that works.

So now you have three estimates:

T(o) = 3 months

T(p) = 30 months

T(m) = 10 months

How would you calculate T(e)? First, let's look at a typical time estimate curve. In most cases, T(o) is closer to T(m) than T(p) is, since there's a limit to how small T(o) can be (T(o)>0), but no real limit to how large T(p) can be (see fig. 6.1).

Situations vary, of course, but usually the worst case is farther away from the most likely than the best case is.

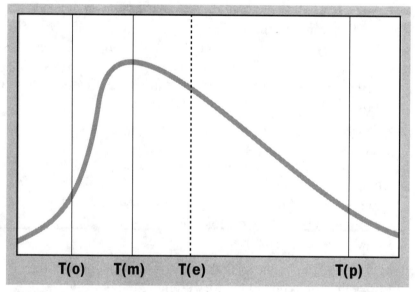

Fig. 6.1. *The best case—T(o)—is usually closer to T(m) than the worst case—T(p)—is.*

Even though the curve in figure 6.1 shows the shape of the time distribution, it doesn't reflect the relative probability of T(o) and T(p) actually happening. Although Murphy's Law would indicate

that T(p) is more probable than T(o), it really isn't. You don't
know the relative probability. On all tasks in all projects, the
relative probability of the extremes should be about even. This
gives the standard bell curve distribution.

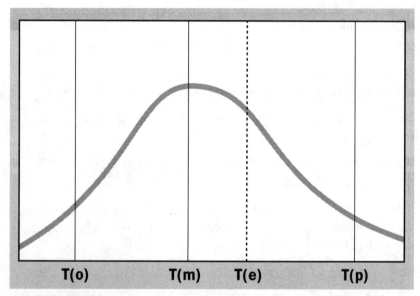

Fig. 6.2. *Although you don't know the relative probability of T(p) or T(o)
occurring, it should be even for the extremes. This produces a bell-shaped
distribution.*

In the standard bell curve distribution, T(m) is given a weight of
4. From that, you can create this weighted average formula
for T(e):

$$T(e) = \frac{T(o) + (4*T(m)) + T(p)}{6}$$

In the engineer's situation, T(e) = $3+(4*10)+\frac{30}{6}$, or $\frac{73}{6}$, which is $12\frac{1}{6}$
months. Depending on the level of precision you want in your
estimate, you might choose to round the T(e) value to 12 months.

"Wait just a minute!" the engineer says. "Why is $12\frac{1}{6}$ months any more valid an estimate than 10 months, or 15 months, for that matter? Isn't this just a SWAG?"

While WAGs and SWAGs are legitimate project estimating tools, this is neither. If there were only one task in the entire project, then, of course, the $12\frac{1}{6}$ months estimate would be clearly nonsense. However, the sample project has numerous tasks.

Let's say there are 6,000 different tasks in the project. Is it likely that at least some tasks will have good luck? Yes, of course.

Is it equally likely that at least some tasks will have bad luck? Equally, yes.

Would you expect most tasks to finish up at more or less their most likely time estimates? Probably.

That's why this technique of calculating T(e) is so powerful. We may not know *which* tasks will have good or bad luck, but we do know that *some* tasks will have good and bad luck.

That allows us to bring probability theory—statistics—into play.

You can safely predict that of a large number of tasks, some will naturally trend toward T(o), some toward T(p), and most toward T(m). You don't know which ones, of course. By using the T(e) estimating formula for each task in a project, that means that while individual task times will fluctuate between the T(o) and T(p) extremes, the impact of that fluctuation will dampen out somewhat. The total project estimate is therefore more solid, even counting the real uncertainty on a task-by-task basis.

Why not just pad the project schedule and be done with it? First, because it's not honest. Second, because you don't know how much to; pad unless you use this technique. (Then it's not padding; it's proper allowance for unpredictable contingencies—totally legitimate and appropriate.)

Third, you get into the "liar's contest" with your boss or client. That's when you always add two weeks to each estimate to be on the safe side. Your boss learns this and automatically cuts two weeks off any time estimate you submit. So you start adding four. That way adds madness—or dismissal.

Special Note for Math-Phobia Sufferers

This is the heavy mathematics portion of the book. After this section, you will do nothing more difficult than basic arithmetic. So, do you have to do this part at all?

Not every project manager must do this. Whether you should work to master this method depends on two things: how uncertain your task estimates are and how important it is that you give an absolutely solid estimate. If your task estimates are certain and your deadline is flexible, and if the statistics don't work easily for you, skip this section altogether.

Warning! You should either calculate T(e) for each task in your project or none of the tasks in your project—don't "mix and match" if you want a total estimate that has some statistical validity.

Confidence Levels and the Standard Deviation

The PERT time estimating technique also helps determine confidence level, which is the probability that you will actually accomplish the task on schedule or within a certain variance.

To determine confidence, you need to know how to calculate the standard deviation, which is represented by the Greek letter sigma (σ):

$$\sigma = \frac{T(p) - T(o)}{6}$$

In the engineer's scenario, $\sigma = \frac{(30-3)}{6}$, or $\frac{27}{6}$, or $4\frac{1}{2}$ months.

A long-standing empirical rule says that when you have a nearly symmetric mound-shaped data set (a bell curve), the following probabilities apply:

- 68.26 percent of the time the work will be completed $\pm$ 1 σ of T(e)

- 95.44 percent of the time the work will be completed $\pm$ 2 σ of T(e)

- 99.73 percent of the time the work will be completed $\pm$ 3 σ of T(e)

Risk and Standard Deviation

Standard deviation can be used as a measure of risk. A large sigma (σ) value on a task is a high-risk task; a small σ value shows a small risk. Since σ shows the range between the pessimistic and optimistic cases, a large spread means there is greater consequence of task failure than a small spread.

In the engineer's scenario, the following confidence levels exist:

Table 6.1 Confidence Measurement

Task	T(o)	T(m)	T(p)	T(e)	σ
Design Guidance System	3	10	30	12.17	4.5

Confidence	Low	High
± 1 σ (68.26%)	7.67	16.67
± 2 σ (95.44%)	3.17	21.17
± 3 σ (99.73%)	3.00	25.67

Note: At 3 σ, the "Low" calculated value is actually 12.17-(3*4.5), or -1.33. Notice that there is no way the "Low" value could actually be lower than T(o), so the T(o) value is just substituted here. Equally, if the "High" value should exceed T(p), substitute the T(p) value.

Since early completion is normally less of a problem than late completion, the engineer can round this off and be 68 percent confident of finishing in no more than $16\frac{2}{3}$ months and 95 percent confident of finishing in no more than $21\frac{1}{6}$ months. (Normally, there is no real value in going to the 3 σ level, since 95 percent confident is high enough for most situations.) This is a very useful technique when you must absolutely finish a job at a certain time or else. Just add 2 σ to T(e) and back up your start date accordingly. (Again, round fractional answers to the nearest sensible time units.)

Armed with a standard statistical table, you can also work backwards, calculating a confidence probability (how likely you are to finish on or before that time) for any given amount of time based on what fraction of a standard deviation the deadline represents.

Standard Deviation for a Task Sequence

There is one extra element involved in standard deviation: how to determine sigma (σ) for a sequence of tasks. Consider the situation depicted in figure 6.3.

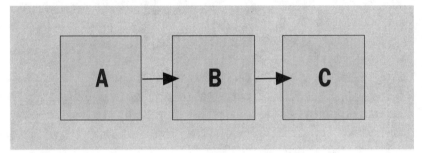

Fig. 6.3. *In this task dependency sequence, starting Task B is dependent upon finishing Task A, and starting Task C is dependent on finishing Task B.*

In project management language, you would describe figure 6.3 by saying that Task B is dependent upon Task A (it can't begin until Task A is finished) and that Task C is dependent upon Task B. How long would it take to complete Tasks A, B, and C in sequence?

Table 6.2   Time Values for Task Completion

Task	T(o)	T(m)	T(p)	T(e)	σ
A	2.00	5.00	9.00	5.17	1.17
B	3.00	7.00	21.00	8.67	3.00
C	1.00	2.00	3.00	2.00	0.33

Task	T(e)	σ	σ^2
A	5.17	1.17	1.36
B	8.67	3.00	9.00
C	2.00	0.33	0.11

Using the values in Table 6.2, the total time for Tasks A, B, and C is equal to the sum of T(e) for A, B, C, which works out to 15.84 weeks.

What, then, is the standard deviation for A, B, C? At first glance, it looks like 4.5, which is the answer when you add up the σ values. But that can't be the answer, since the chance of all three tasks running late must be less than the chance of any one task running late. If 4.5 is too high, the average sigma (σ) value (1.5) is too small, since the standard deviation must be greater than the greatest individual σ value.

To calculate the sigma (σ) value for A, B, C, you must first square the standard deviations for each task, add them up, and then take the square root of the sum (the square root of the sum of the squares).

Table 6.3 **Time Estimate With Confidence Factors**

Sum of T(e)	15.84
Sum of Squares of Std. Dev.	10.48
Square Root of Sum of Squares	3.24
68% Confidence (±1 std. dev.)	19.08
95% Confidence (±2 std. dev.)	22.31
99% Confidence (±3 std. dev.)	25.55

This sounds more complicated than it is. You have already calculated T(e) and sigma (σ) for each task. Armed with a spreadsheet program, squaring the standard deviations is a simple matter. Once you know the order in which you will perform the tasks (you got this from your Sticky Note PERT chart), list the tasks in sequence and add up the squares of the standard deviation. Take the square root of the sum, which involves pushing only one button on your calculator—or setting up your spreadsheet to do the calculation automatically. For the desired degree of confidence, add in the number of standard deviations you wish (one or two in most cases). Voila! You have a valid estimate with confidence factors. (See Table 6.3.) Round the numbers to the nearest sensible time units: 3.24 is either $3\frac{1}{4}$ or 3; 22.31 is either $22\frac{1}{4}$ or 22.

Crash Time and the CPM Method

Consider this example of simultaneous invention: Around the time the PERT system was developed, DuPont and Remington Rand developed CPM, the **C**ritical **P**ath **M**ethod. CPM, like PERT, uses a network approach for large project management. With both tools available to them, project managers began almost at once to use their favorite elements of both PERT and CPM, with the practical result that PERT and CPM today are used effectively as synonyms. While this statement is not strictly accurate, on an everyday level, it might as well be. Most project managers use a hybrid of the two systems and call the resulting system whatever they like.

There are some important differences between PERT and CPM, one of which is the CPM technique for time estimating, called crash time. *Crash time* is the fastest time in which a task can be accomplished *given unlimited resources.*

Please note that additional resources don't always speed up a task. If it takes one woman nine months to have a baby, it doesn't mean that nine women could do the job in only one. In addition, watch out for the "too many cooks spoil the broth" problem. Two people might speed up a task, but twenty would likely slow it down.

Return to the Polaris example with the guidance system engineer. Recall your initial request: "I need a guidance system for the new ICBM that will allow us to shoot the missile from under water anywhere in the world, then travel 3,000 miles to its destination and land within 100 yards of its target. Nothing like this has ever been done before. So, how long will it take you?"

This time, the engineer looks at you slyly. "I don't know. How many people do I get to help me do this?"

The engineer realizes that the actual time to complete many tasks is dependent on the resources available to do the work. In this scenario, there are many different approaches the engineer can take. The engineer can try one approach at a time until the right one is found, or can lead simultaneous teams on each approach until the right one is found. The tradeoff is time versus resources. In other words, you might be able to "buy" a time very close to T(o), given enough staff and money. How do you decide what makes sense?

Before you analyze the situation further, you must understand two concepts related to crash time: crash cost and crash slope (see fig. 6.4).

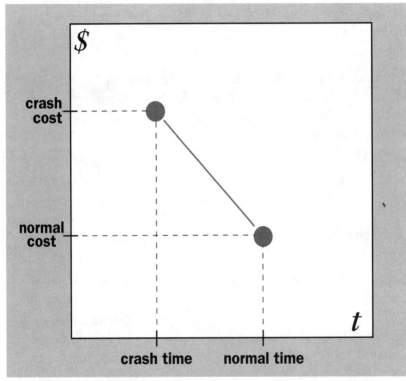

Fig. 6.4. *Crash analysis is a way of estimating the effect of applying additional resources to a project.*

Crash cost is the total cost of the resources necessary to achieve the crash time.

Crash slope is actually two numbers. First, it's the difference between the crash time and the normal time. Second, it's the difference between the crash cost and the normal cost. There can be different points on the crash slope, because there can be different scenarios of resources versus time.

Going back to the Polaris example, follow these steps to decide the tradeoff between time and resources.

Step 1: *Determine normal time.*

Let's make the normal time for one engineer the PERT estimate, about 12 months.

Step 2: *Determine crash time.*

Hypothetically, let's conclude that three engineers (supervisor and two staff) could cut the time to six months, and that five engineers (supervisor and four staff) could cut the time to four months. Beyond that, you decide that extra staff won't yield significant additional time savings.

Step 3: *Determine normal cost.*

The senior engineer makes about $5,000 a month, making the normal staff cost $60,000.

Step 4: *Determine crash cost.*

If staff engineers make $4,000 a month, the three-engineer/6-month version will cost $78,000, and the five-engineer/4-month version will cost $84,000.

Step 5: *Determine crash slope.*

For three engineers, the time savings is six months and the additional cost is $18,000. The crash slope is normally written in parentheses, thus: (-6, $18,000). For five engineers, the crash slope is (-8, $24,000).

Step 6: *Determine whether it's worth it.*

You can probably imagine a situation in which a time savings of six months is easily worth $18,000 and another in which it wouldn't be worthwhile. In this example, you'll need more information about the project layout before you can definitely decide which scenario makes most sense. Right now, the benefit is knowing about one more option for better managing project tradeoffs. Chapter 8 will return to this issue.

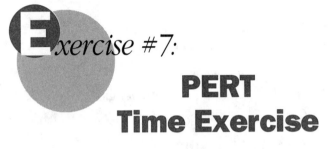

xercise #7:

PERT
Time Exercise

The easiest way to complete this exercise is to use a spreadsheet program. Set up the information shown in the table on the next page. Then calculate T(e), σ, and σ^2 for all the tasks A through J.

Next, assume that there's a sequence of tasks, A, C, E, F, and G, to be completed in that order.

- What is the T(e) for all those tasks?
- What is the sum of the squares of the standard deviations of the individual tasks?
- What is the standard deviation of the path sequence (the square root of the sum of the squares)?

Write your answers in the boxes provided in the table.

Task	T(o)	T(m)	T(p)	T(e)	σ	σ²
A	2.00	5.00	9.00			
B	3.00	7.00	21.00			
C	1.00	2.00	3.00			
D	4.00	6.00	20.00			
E	2.00	3.00	7.00			
F	3.00	9.00	25.00			
G	5.00	12.00	18.00			
H	3.00	10.00	11.00			
I	1.00	2.00	6.00			
J	2.00	4.00	9.00			

For Tasks A, C, E, F, G

T(e)	
$\sum \sigma^2$	
σ	

Formulas:

$$T(e) = \frac{T(o) + (4 * T(m)) + T(p)}{6}$$

$$\sigma = \frac{T(p) - T(o)}{6}$$

Answers for Exercise #7

Task	T(o)	T(m)	T(p)	T(e)	σ	σ²
A	2.00	5.00	9.00	5.17	1.17	1.36
B	3.00	7.00	21.00	8.67	3.00	9.00
C	1.00	2.00	3.00	2.00	0.33	0.11
D	4.00	6.00	20.00	8.00	2.67	7.11
E	2.00	3.00	7.00	3.50	0.83	0.69
F	3.00	9.00	25.00	10.67	3.67	13.44
G	5.00	12.00	18.00	11.83	2.17	4.69
H	3.00	10.00	11.00	9.00	1.33	1.78
I	1.00	2.00	6.00	2.50	0.83	0.69
J	2.00	4.00	9.00	4.50	1.17	1.36

For Tasks A, C, E, F, G

T(e)	33.17
$\sum \sigma^2$	20.31
σ	4.506

How to Make and Use a Gantt Chart

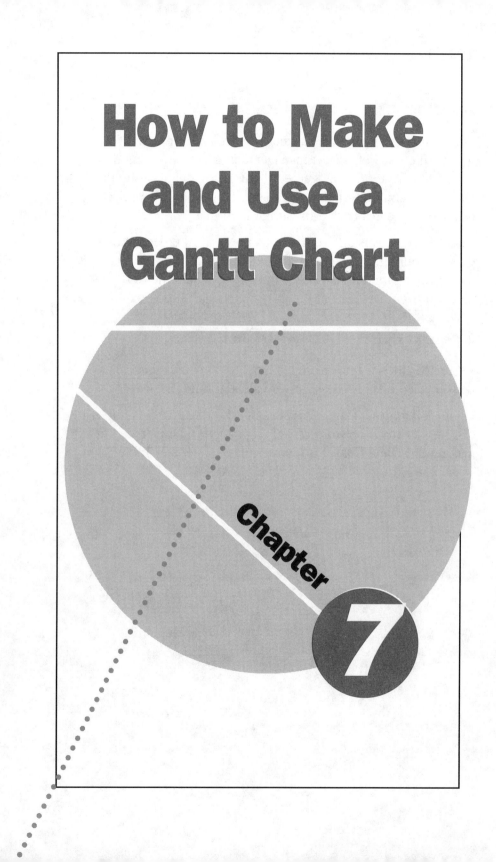

Chapter

7

Although people have been managing projects throughout history, the tools of project management are mostly of modern origin. In Chapter 6, you learned that the beginning of the PERT and CPM techniques dates back to the 1950s. Modern project management dates back a bit farther than that.

Henry L. Gantt was an ordinance engineer at Aberdeen Proving Grounds during World War I. His contribution to modern project management, the eponymous Gantt Chart, is still one of the most practical everyday tools in the project manager's toolbox.

How to Draw a Gantt Chart

A Gantt Chart is a simple project timeline. It shows the performance of project tasks over calendar time.

Figure 7.1 shows a Gantt Chart based on the exercise example in Chapter 4: buying a word processing system. The first step in making this Gantt Chart is to create a task table (see Table 7.1).

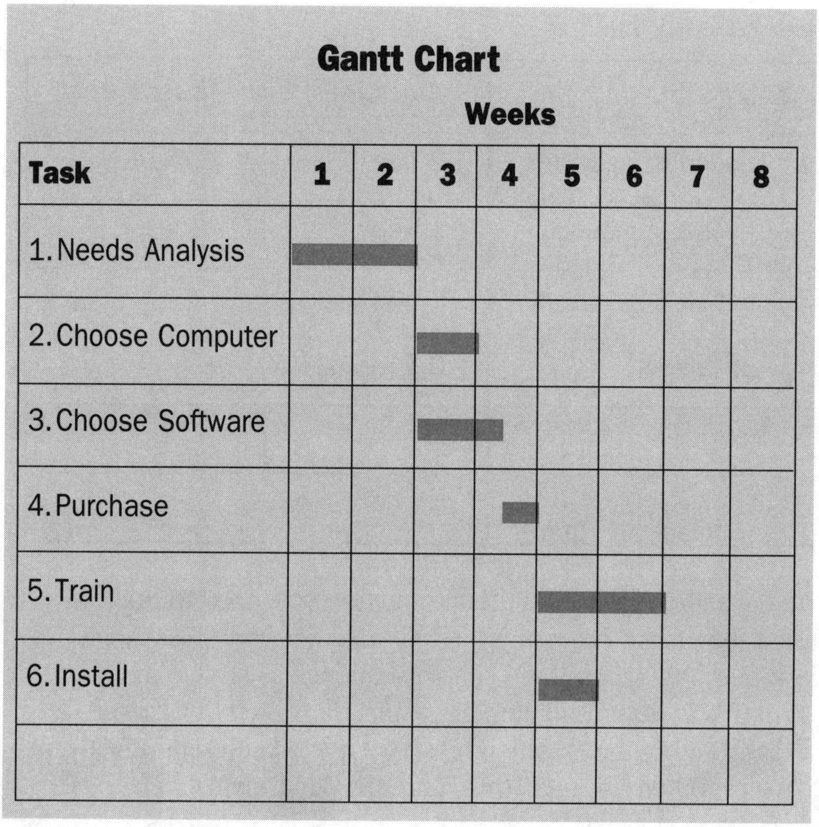

Gantt Chart

Weeks

Task	1	2	3	4	5	6	7	8
1. Needs Analysis	▬	▬						
2. Choose Computer			▬					
3. Choose Software			▬					
4. Purchase				▬				
5. Train					▬	▬		
6. Install					▬			

Fig. 7.1. *A Gantt Chart showing the tasks involved in buying a word processor.*

Table 7.1 **Task Table**

Task	Duration	Dependency
1. Needs Analysis	2 weeks	N/A
2. Choose Computer	1 week	1
3. Choose Software	1.5 weeks	1
4. Purchase	0.5 weeks	2, 3
5. Train User	2 weeks	4
6. Install System	1 week	4

You have already created the information you need to build a Task Table in the process of putting together your Task Analysis worksheets: the Task ID (a simple sequence as shown in Table 7.1, or a WBS-based numbering system as shown in Chapter 5), the Task Name, the Duration [use T(e) if you are doing PERT time estimates; otherwise use T(m)], and the Dependency Relationship (what follows what).

The first task, "Needs Analysis," begins the project, so nothing is dependent upon it. "Needs Analysis" starts at the beginning of the project (beginning of Week 1) and lasts for two weeks.

Two tasks, "Choose Computer" and "Choose Software," share the same dependency: both are waiting for "Needs Analysis" to finish. Therefore, both Gantt Chart bars begin in the week following the end of "Needs Analysis." Since the two tasks don't have the same duration, the bars aren't the same length.

The fourth task, "Purchase," is dependent upon both "Choose Computer" and "Choose Software." That means it cannot begin until both predecessors are complete. Even though "Choose Computer" is finished at the end of Week 3, "Purchasing" can't begin because there's still half a week to go before "Choose Software" is scheduled to finish. *When one task has multiple predecessors, its earliest start is after the end of its latest predecessor.*

Finally, "Train" and "Install" are both dependent upon "Purchase." They follow the same process as Tasks 2 and 3, above.

As long as you make a Task Table first and follow the dependency sequence, you'll find drawing Gantt Charts quite easy.

Let's prepare a Gantt Chart for installing a LAN. First, prepare a Task Table, using T(e) values (see Table 7.2).

Using a spreadsheet program, you can set up formulas to automatically calculate T(e) and σ for each task when you enter T(o), T(p), and T(m).

Tip! You'll notice that the T(e) and σ values keep turning out to be numbers like "2.27 weeks." This quickly turns silly. Round them to the nearest sensible time unit. For this example, they are rounded to the nearest full day (using days rather than weeks as the standard time unit), resulting in the data in Table 7.3.

Table 7.2 Task Table for Installing a LAN

No.	Task	T(o)	T(p)	T(m)	T(e)	σ	Dependent On...
1	Project Mgmt.	8.80	36.00	14.40	17.07	4.53	N/A
2	Needs Analysis	1.60	4.00	2.00	2.27	0.40	N/A
3	Specifications	1.00	3.00	1.00	1.33	0.33	2
4	Select Server	1.00	2.00	1.60	1.57	0.17	3
5	Select Software	1.00	4.00	3.00	2.83	0.50	3
6	Select Cables	0.20	1.40	1.00	0.93	0.20	4
7	Purchasing	0.20	3.00	0.40	0.80	0.47	5, 6
8	Manuals	2.00	4.00	3.00	3.00	0.33	7
9	Wire Offices	3.00	9.00	4.00	4.67	1.00	7
10	Set Up Server	0.40	2.00	1.00	1.07	0.27	7
11	Dev. Training	2.00	4.60	3.00	3.10	0.43	8
12	Install Software	0.40	1.60	1.00	1.00	0.20	10
13	Connect Network	0.40	2.00	1.00	1.07	0.27	9, 12
14	Train Users	2.00	2.00	2.00	2.00	0.00	11, 13
15	Test/Debug	1.00	9.00	2.00	3.00	1.33	13
16	Acceptance	0.60	2.00	1.00	1.10	0.23	14, 15

Table 7.3 Task Table With Times Rounded to Nearest Unit

No.	Task	T(o)	T(p)	T(m)	T(e)	σ	Dependent On...
1	Project Mgmt.	44	180	72	85	23	N/A
2	Needs Analysis	8	20	10	11	2	N/A
3	Specifications	5	15	5	7	2	2
4	Select Server	5	10	8	8	1	3
5	Select Software	5	20	15	14	3	3
6	Select Cables	1	7	5	5	1	4
7	Purchasing	1	15	2	4	2	5, 6
8	Manuals	10	20	15	15	2	7
9	Wire Offices	15	45	20	23	5	7
10	Set Up Server	2	10	5	5	1	7
11	Dev. Training	10	23	15	16	2	8
12	Install Software	2	8	5	5	1	10
13	Connect Network	2	10	5	5	1	9, 12
14	Train Users	10	10	10	10	0	11, 13
15	Test/Debug	5	45	10	15	7	13
16	Acceptance	3	10	5	6	1	14, 15

The only tricky part here is coming up with time estimates for Task 1, "Project Management." You need to know how to determine the Critical Path, which will be covered in detail in the next chapter. As a quick preview, to calculate the time for "Project Management," you have to put the task times in the Sticky Note PERT outline (see fig. 4.2). You need to look for the longest path, and add up the times for those tasks. In other words, the time it takes to manage the project is equal to the time the project itself takes. The longest path in your project is called the *Critical Path*.

Armed with the Task Table, the next job is to draw the Gantt Chart itself. The Gantt Chart in figure 7.2 was drawn by project management software rather than by hand. (For a brief discussion of the pros and cons of project management software, see the accompanying sidebar, titled "Computers and Project Management.")

As you study the Gantt Chart of the sample project, remember that the project was due in 16 weeks, or by the end of the fiscal year (September 30, let's assume). According to the draft Gantt Chart, the project will be finished at the end of the week of October 1— a week behind schedule! (You could also determine this by looking at the duration of the Project Management task. If there are 80 available days—16 weeks—and the estimated duration is 85 days, the project clearly is not on track for the planned deadline.)

Has a mistake been made? Not at all. It's extremely difficult to see how long a project will take until the Task Table is prepared and the first Gantt Chart is drawn. The odds are that your first draft will tend to be over-deadline. Don't worry—no Gantt Chart is ever wrong until it's the version you make official.

The job now is to see how you can shorten the duration of the project without affecting quality.

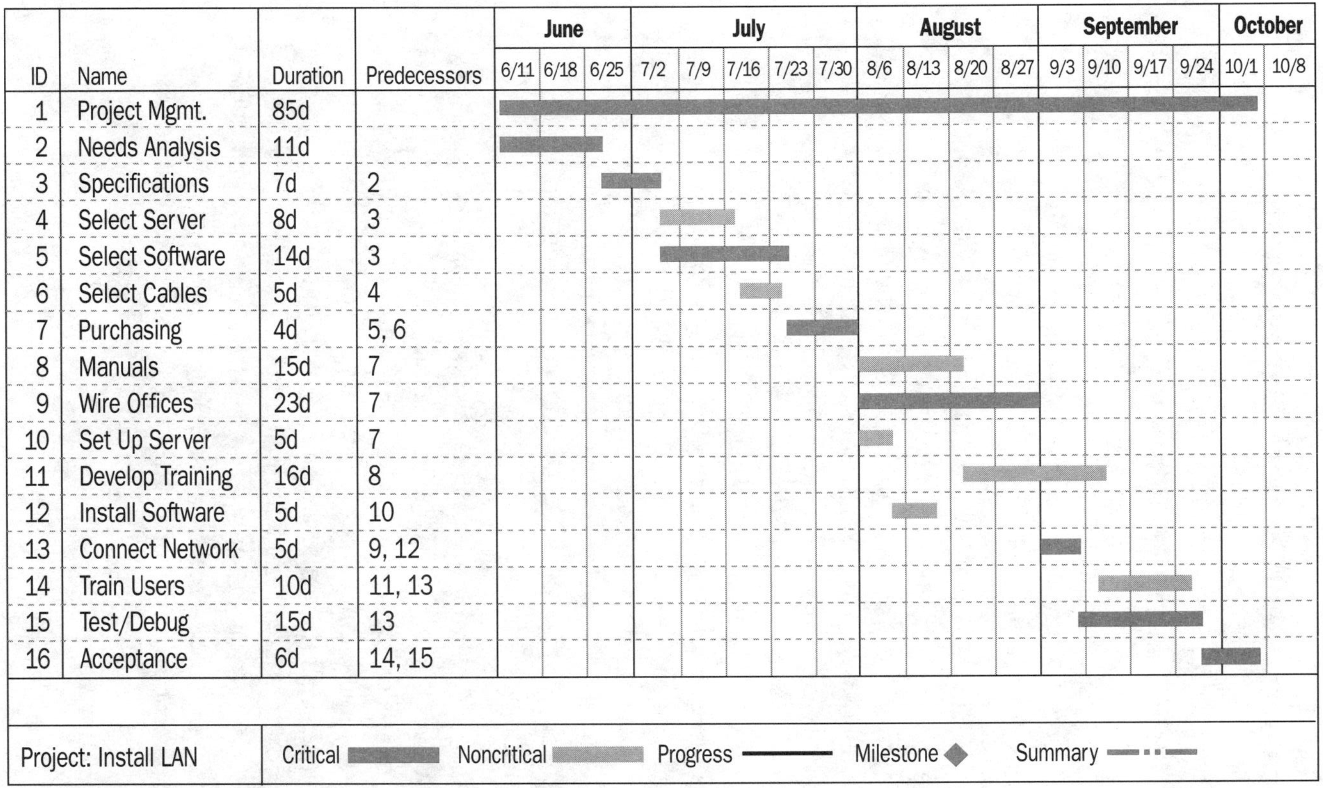

ID
Name
Duration
Predecessors
June
July
August
September
October
6/11 6/18 6/25 7/2 7/9 7/16 7/23 7/30 8/6 8/13 8/20 8/27 9/3 9/10 9/17 9/24 10/1 10/8
1 Project Mgmt. 85d
2 Needs Analysis 11d
3 Specifications 7d 2
4 Select Server 8d 3
5 Select Software 14d 3
6 Select Cables 5d 4
7 Purchasing 4d 5, 6
8 Manuals 15d 7
9 Wire Offices 23d 7
10 Set Up Server 5d 7
11 Develop Training 16d 8
12 Install Software 5d 10
13 Connect Network 5d 9, 12
14 Train Users 10d 11, 13
15 Test/Debug 15d 13
16 Acceptance 6d 14, 15
Project: Install LAN
Critical
Noncritical
Progress
Milestone
Summary

Fig. 7.2. *A Gantt Chart for installing a LAN, drawn with project management software.*

Computers and Project Management

"If you don't have a problem, don't try to fix it with a computer." This is always good advice, but particularly important in the area of project management software, which once won a category award in a computer magazine for "type of software most often purchased merely to sit unopened on the shelf."

In the same way that a word processing system is of little use to someone who can't read, project management software is of absolutely no use to someone who doesn't know how to create Gantt Charts and other tools by hand. If you know how to use the tools already, then a computer can speed up the work, do your arithmetic, keep good records, and draw your diagrams more neatly. While these are considerable benefits, they are not "project management." Project management is what project managers do, not what software does. It would be more accurate to say that there is no such thing as project management software—rather, there is only "project tracking and scheduling" software.

This book will use the conventional name for the category, however. Project management software will do some or all of the following: create Gantt, PERT, and CPM charts from Task Table information (you still have to do the task table yourself), allow you to assign resources to tasks, keep track of your resource scheduling, alert you to conflicts between resource availability and workload, track resources allocated among projects, create task lists, show actual versus plan in task accomplishment, calculate the Critical Path, and more. Ease of updating and the ability to look at multiple options are other advantages.

Project management software has a reputation for requiring a significant learning curve, but that's partly because some people buy project management software because they don't know how to manage their projects. This is a mistake, though not one you can blame on the software itself. You're better off studying project management first, gaining familiarity with the tools, and then using software packages to speed up the work and improve your accuracy.

The availability and "user-friendliness" of project management software have improved remarkably over the last several years. Many project managers who previously would have found software to be overkill as a tool now find it useful. This book can't make specific package recommendations for several reasons: individual needs and preferences differ, size and complexity of projects differ, and any recommendation that's valid today would be obsolete in short order.

Do your homework by reading test reports in leading computer magazines, analyze your needs, and shop accordingly. Don't pay primary attention to the price of the package; the least expensive part of using software is the cost of the software itself. Most of the real cost will be user time.

Project management software packages do fall into some rough categories. These are power categories, not quality categories.

Major projects. For the very largest of projects ($10 million+), you can get comprehensive packages that run on mainframes and networks. Primavera is a well-known package in this category. Although it comes in a Windows-based version, the comprehensive Primavera package has numerous modules and add-ons and can cost more than $100,000 for a full implementation. If you're running 15,000 tasks on a $4 billion project, this may be a bargain; if you're running 20 tasks on a $5,000 project, it's clearly a little excessive.

Medium projects. The most popular category of project management software includes titles like Workbench, Timeline, SuperProject, and Microsoft Project. (Microsoft Project was used in the preparation of this book.) This category of full-featured programs allows you to manage projects of up to 1,000 to 1,500 tasks comfortably. Most carry street prices ranging from $400 to $700.

Small projects. For basic Gantt Charting, small projects, or project managers who don't want to do resource planning in software, numerous packages, including FastTrack Scheduler, InstaPlan 5000, and OnTarget, are available. Some organizer software packages and personal information managers (PIMs) now include basic Gantt Chart functions. There's even some shareware (EasyProject) that works at this level.

Non-project management software. "If the only tool you have is a hammer, all problems look like nails." Use the right tools for the job. In addition to formal "project management" software, consider using spreadsheets, drawing programs, flowcharters, and other tools.

Ways to Shorten a Project Schedule

There are many different approaches you can take to shorten a project schedule. Currently, the sample project has a duration of 85 days, with 80 days as the goal. That means you need to cut roughly five days from the project—not a big deal. But wait! Before finalizing this, let's calculate the sigma (σ) of the project, which is the σ of the Critical (longest) Path (the darker bars on the Gantt Chart, which were automatically calculated by the program—another bonus for using software). To calculate the σ, square the standard deviations of the tasks, add them together, and take the square root of the sum. This gives a σ of 9.54 days. To be 95 percent confident of meeting the end-of-fiscal-year deadline, add 2σ to the total duration, for 104 working days. That would be the ideal length of time for this project, which means you need to cut 24 days from the current 85. (See Table 7.4.)

What if you can't? It's not a catastrophe if you can't find a way to cut 24 days, but you must cut a minimum of 5 days to get to the 80-day target. Cutting all 24 days gives you a 95 percent chance of meeting the goal regardless of problems, but you're paid to manage the problems.

As you examine the sample project for ways to cut time, consider these three methods:

- Adding resources to critical tasks

- Changing task sequence

- Reducing the project/task scope

Table 7.4 **Total Project Duration**

Task	T(e)	σ	σ²
Needs Analysis	11.33	2.00	4.00
Specifications	6.67	1.67	2.78
Select Software	14.17	2.50	6.25
Purchasing	4.00	2.33	5.44
Wire Offices	23.33	5.00	25.00
Connect Network	5.33	1.33	1.78
Test/Debug	15.00	6.67	44.44
Acceptance	5.50	1.17	1.36
Totals	85.33		91.06
Square Root of std. dev.		=	9.54
2 σ		=	19.08
95% Confidence	104 days		
Available	80 days		
NEED TO CUT	24 days		

1. **Add resources to critical tasks.** Apply the CPM crash time concept—additional resources can shorten some tasks. Apply crash time only to tasks where speeding them up actually shortens the project: follow the task sequence to the end to make sure. (*Tip!* If a task is "noncritical"—that is, not on the longest path—we say it has "slack"—extra time to complete it before it bumps into the next task. For a fuller discussion of "slack," see page 171. Notice that if you "crash" such a task, the project isn't going to finish any quicker.) Resources can be extra team members, outside contractors, staff borrowed from other departments, or even overtime.

Add one person to "Wire Offices." That's a 50 percent staff increase, which should (you hope!) speed up the project by at least 50 percent. [Take the 50 percent off T(o) and T(m), but take only 25 percent off T(p).] Also buy some consulting services to help with both "Set Up Server" and "Install Software." Doing so should reduce each task by about a week. (Budget implications will be dealt with later; remember, time is the driver.)

2. **Change task sequence.** When you created the original Sticky Note PERT chart, you made various decisions about task sequence. How you sequence your tasks has a dramatic impact on total project duration. Consider alternatives that might be shorter. Don't forget ways to forge a dependency sequence other than FS—especially overlaps.

   For this example, overlap "Specifications" with "Needs Analysis" by five days. If you consider that needs analysis will be done in sections, you can start developing specifications for each section as it is completed. Also, you can start writing the manuals as soon as you decide on the software and hardware; you don't have to wait for "Purchasing" to be completed.

3. **Reduce the project/task scope.** You can speed up a task if you do less work. Do you need all the planned features? Is it necessary to your driver that the entire wish list be included? If you can redefine the work in a way that doesn't interfere with fundamental quality issues, you can speed up the project.

   For this example, plan on being less comprehensive in manual development and rely much more on existing commercial documentation. As an alternative to creating a full-fledged manual, you can issue a "Frequently Asked Questions" report after the system is on-line, which you'd probably need to do in any case. That should cut manual preparation time in half.

Also contract out most of the "Develop Training" task to a commercial vendor that offers generic training in LAN operations. You would then need to do just a one-day workshop on your company's unique issues, which should cut "Develop Training" time by more than half.

Table 7.5 Task Table Resulting From Actions to Shorten Project

No.	Task	T(o)	T(p)	T(m)	T(e)	σ	Dependent On...
1	Project Mgmt.	6.30	32.75	11.40	14.11	4.41	N/A
2	Needs Analysis	1.60	4.00	2.00	2.27	0.40	N/A
3	Specifications	1.00	3.00	1.00	1.33	0.33	2, overlap 1 week
4	Select Server	1.00	2.00	1.60	1.57	0.17	3
5	Select Software	1.00	4.00	3.00	2.83	0.50	3
6	Select Cables	0.20	1.40	1.00	0.93	0.20	4
7	Purchasing	0.20	3.00	0.40	0.80	0.47	5, 6
8	Manuals	1.00	2.00	1.50	1.50	0.17	5, 6
9	Wire Offices	1.50	6.75	2.00	2.71	0.88	7
10	Set Up Server	0.40	2.00	1.00	1.07	0.27	7
11	Dev. Training	2.00	4.60	3.00	3.10	0.43	8
12	Install Software	0.40	1.60	1.00	1.00	0.20	10
13	Connect Network	0.40	2.00	1.00	1.07	0.27	9, 12
14	Train Users	2.00	2.00	2.00	2.00	0.00	11, 13
15	Test/Debug	1.00	9.00	2.00	3.00	1.33	13
16	Acceptance	0.60	2.00	1.00	1.10	0.23	14, 15

If you followed these three recommendations for shortening the project, you would redo the task table as shown in Table 7.5 (see Table 7.6). Then you would round the durations back to the nearest day. (Notice that you wouldn't work from the previously rounded figures; that compounds error. In each case, you return to the original figures.) This cuts the project down to 71 days—9 days under schedule. But based on the 2σ ideal goal, you would

Table 7.6 **Task Table With Durations Rounded to Nearest Day**

No.	Task	T(e)	σ	Dependent On...
1	Project Mgmt.	71	22	N/A
2	Needs Analysis	11	2	N/A
3	Specifications	7	2	2, overlap 5 days
4	Select Server	8	1	3
5	Select Software	14	3	3
6	Select Cables	5	1	4
7	Purchasing	4	2	5, 6
8	Manuals	8	1	5, 6
9	Wire Offices	14	4	7
10	Set Up Server	5	1	7
11	Dev. Training	16	2	8
12	Install Software	5	1	10
13	Connect Network	5	1	9, 12
14	Train Users	10	0	11, 13
15	Test/Debug	15	7	13
16	Acceptance	6	1	14, 15

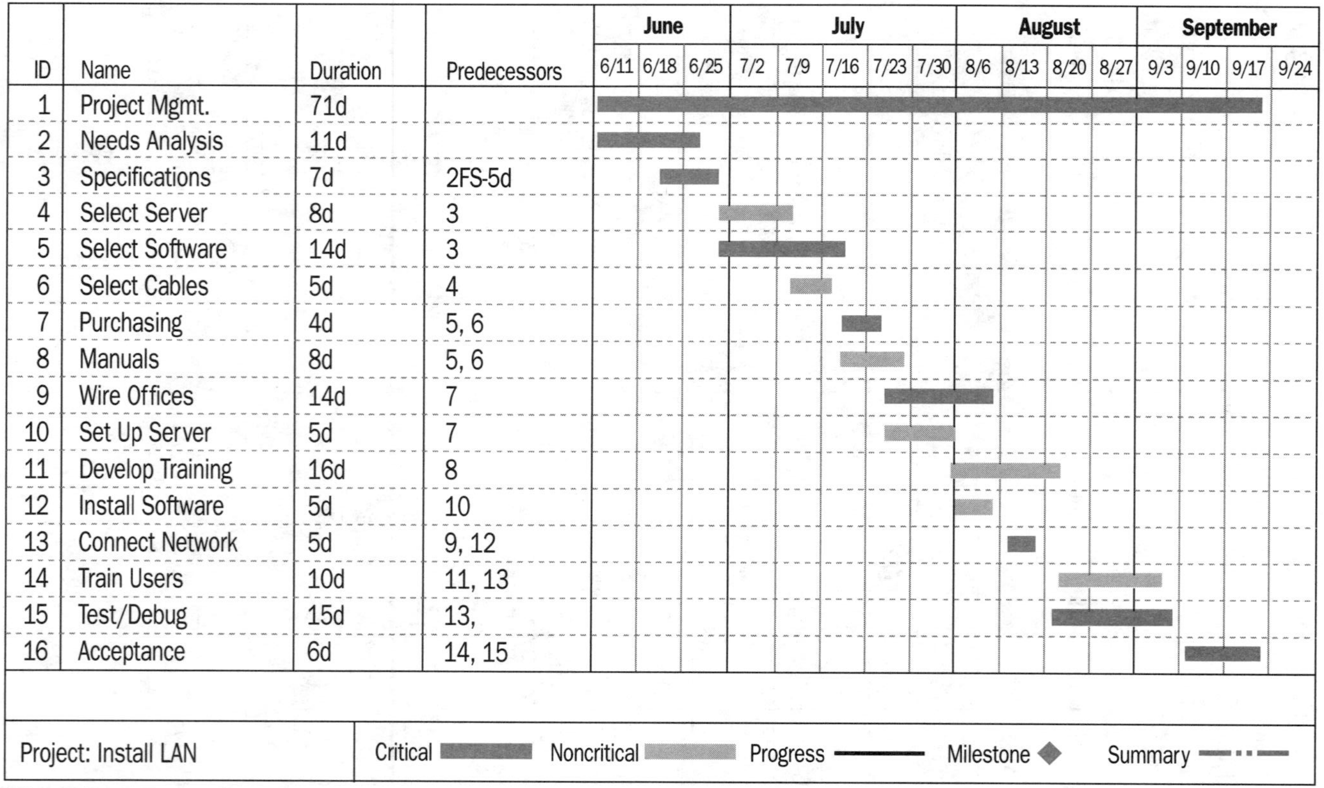

ID	Name	Duration	Predecessors
1	Project Mgmt.	71d	
2	Needs Analysis	11d	
3	Specifications	7d	2FS-5d
4	Select Server	8d	3
5	Select Software	14d	3
6	Select Cables	5d	4
7	Purchasing	4d	5, 6
8	Manuals	8d	5, 6
9	Wire Offices	14d	7
10	Set Up Server	5d	7
11	Develop Training	16d	8
12	Install Software	5d	10
13	Connect Network	5d	9, 12
14	Train Users	10d	11, 13
15	Test/Debug	15d	13,
16	Acceptance	6d	14, 15

Timeline columns — June: 6/11, 6/18, 6/25; July: 7/2, 7/9, 7/16, 7/23, 7/30; August: 8/6, 8/13, 8/20, 8/27; September: 9/3, 9/10, 9/17, 9/24

Project: Install LAN

Legend: Critical — Noncritical — Progress — Milestone ◆ — Summary

Fig. 7.3. A Gantt Chart.

Table 7.7 Total Project Duration

Task	T(e)	σ	σ²
Needs Analysis	11.33	2.00	4.00
Specifications	1.67	1.67	2.78 (-5 days for overlap)
Select Software	14.17	2.50	6.25
Purchasing	4.00	2.33	5.44
Wire Offices	13.54	4.38	19.14
Connect Network	5.33	1.33	1.78
Test/Debug	15.00	6.67	44.44
Acceptance	5.50	1.17	1.36
Totals	70.54		85.20
Square Root of std. dev.		=	9.23
2 σ		=	18.46
95% Confidence	89 days		
Available	80 days		
NEED TO CUT	9 days		

still need 89 days for 95 percent certainty. Since you only have 80, you're somewhere between 67 percent and 95 percent confident of meeting the goal—let's say around 75 percent. That's without extra effort on your part. Figure 7.3 shows a Gantt Chart based on the revised task table, and Table 7.7 shows the total project duration.

(If the math still seems confusing, use this section as a reference guide on your next project. Do each step in the process one at a time, using your project. You'll find that the answers will make better sense to you when they're based on work you have experience with.)

Using a Gantt Chart for Resource Allocation and Resource Management

You can use your Gantt Chart to determine how many people you need on your project team, how they should be scheduled, and how to resolve potential conflicts.

Let's start with the revised sample project Gantt Chart (see fig. 7.4). First, calculate staff requirements using a simplified method, and then you'll learn how to do it in more realistic circumstances.

Make the following assumptions:

1. Each task requires one full-time worker in each week.

2. All team members possess the skills to perform any function.

3. The project manager is a full-time manager and doesn't have to perform any tasks on the project.

Given these assumptions, how many people do you need on the project team?

The way to determine this is to look down each column of the chart, each representing one calendar week. Count the bars down each column, and you'll find the following resource loading for the project. (Note: This was done by hand, not with software. While there is a way to do this with software, the technique varies from program to program.)

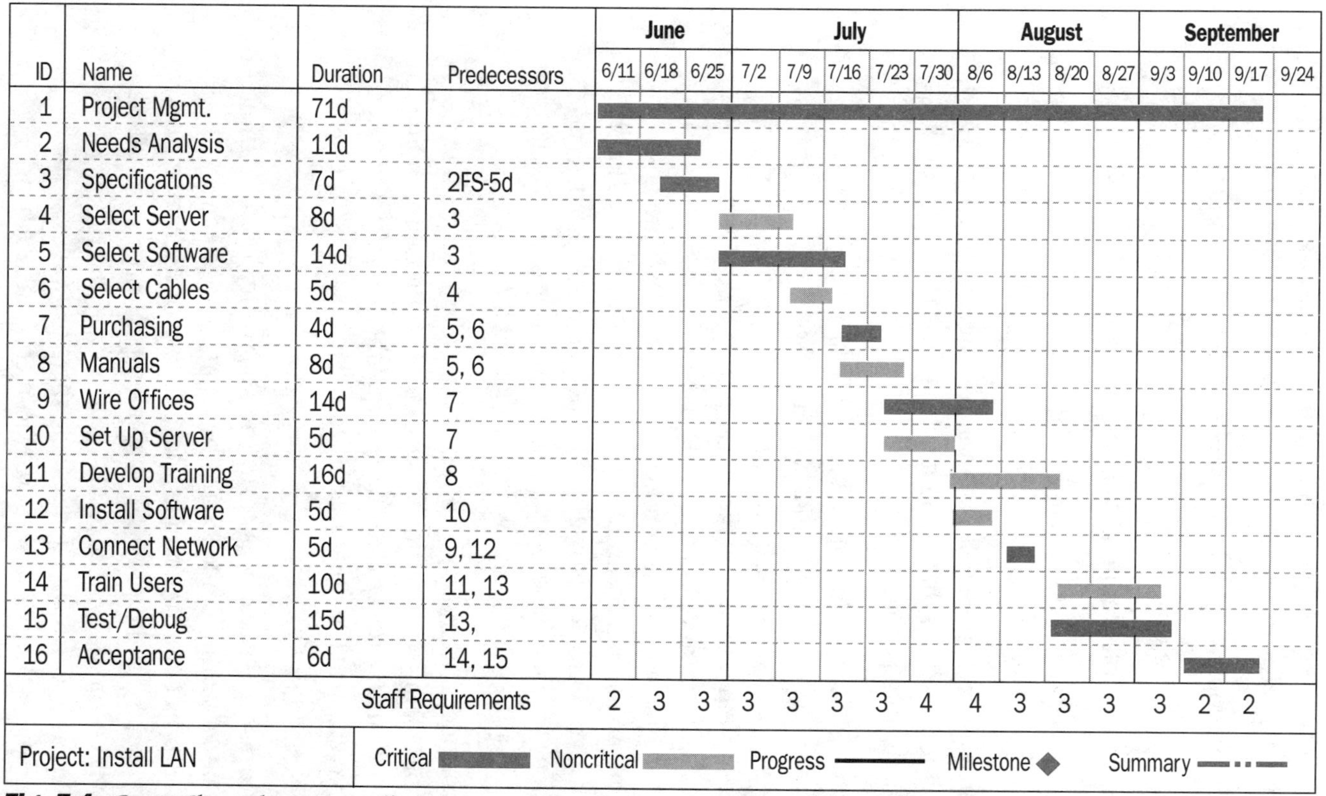

ID	Name	Duration	Predecessors	June 6/11	6/18	6/25	7/2	July 7/9	7/16	7/23	7/30	August 8/6	8/13	8/20	8/27	September 9/3	9/10	9/17	9/24
1	Project Mgmt.	71d																	
2	Needs Analysis	11d																	
3	Specifications	7d	2FS-5d																
4	Select Server	8d	3																
5	Select Software	14d	3																
6	Select Cables	5d	4																
7	Purchasing	4d	5, 6																
8	Manuals	8d	5, 6																
9	Wire Offices	14d	7																
10	Set Up Server	5d	7																
11	Develop Training	16d	8																
12	Install Software	5d	10																
13	Connect Network	5d	9, 12																
14	Train Users	10d	11, 13																
15	Test/Debug	15d	13,																
16	Acceptance	6d	14, 15																
	Staff Requirements			2	3	3	3	3	3	3	4	4	3	3	3	3	3	2	2

Project: Install LAN — Critical ■ Noncritical ■ Progress ▬ Milestone ◆ Summary ▬▬

Fig. 7.4. *Gantt Chart showing staff requirements for each week of the LAN installation project.*

As you can see from the Gantt Chart in figure 7.4, your staff requirements for this project break down as follows:

- Two people during three weeks of the total project
- Four people during two weeks of the project
- Three people during all the remaining weeks

How many people do you need? Two is too few, four is wasteful, and three is sometimes insufficient.

Because three is the most common resource requirement, start with a team size of three, counting the project manager. This brings up two problems.

First, what do you do in the weeks in which you employ more people than you need? Is that wasteful? Not if you are proactive. The extra, or "slack," resources, may be able to do extra work to speed up other tasks. This is an essentially free way to crash-time tasks. Slack resources may also be used to reduce project risk— you have resources you can keep in reserve for emergencies. Or, they may be assigned useful organizational work that doesn't involve your project. However you decide to use your reserves, consider yourself lucky: few project managers ever have to worry about not having enough work for their staff to do.

The second, and more serious, problem with creating a three-member team is what to do in weeks when the staff requirement is greater than project team size. Remember, during two weeks of the project, you'll require four team members. There are two potential solutions:

1. **Adjust the resources to fit the schedule.** There's no rule that all team members must be "start-to-finish" members of the project team. You may have a core of team members who remain with the project throughout its lifespan, and others who come in as needed, either to supplement the team or to supply specialized talents. Plus, there's always overtime— another way to add resources to meet peak demand.

2. Adjust the schedule to fit the resources. This process is known as *leveling*. If there are insufficient resources in a given week, shift the work ahead. Ideally, you will "level within slack"; that is, you first adjust the tasks that already have extra time built into the schedule so you won't jeopardize the entire project schedule. When slack is insufficient to resolve all conflicts, the total schedule begins to slip. When time is not the driver, this may be perfectly satisfactory. *(Tip!* When you're trying to "level within slack," you'll sometimes discover that a given task may be split: one section may be done first, then another task may intervene, and then the remaining part of the first task may be finished.)

Of course, the simple assumptions used here to demonstrate this method don't apply in every real-world situation. Some tasks require more than one staff member, some less than forty hours in a week.

You can still calculate resource loading requirements for each period of your project. Add each bar in the Gantt Chart for the number of team members required each week (fractions for less than full-time work), just as you did before.

What about the other assumption: that all project team members possess all necessary skills?

To resolve this conflict, you have to schedule work to people. Let's return to the original one-staff one-task assumption, but this time assume that not everyone has all the necessary skills.

The core team consists of Bill Mata, Project Manager, and staff members Bob Hancock and Rey Harter. Assume that Claudia Geary will be used as a temporary resource for overload weeks.

In addition to the Project Gantt Charts you've been doing so far, you can also prepare a Resource Gantt Chart that shows the assignments of a resource over time. (This is handy not only as a management and control device, but also when a single resource is scheduled across multiple projects. Many of the midrange software packages will produce this kind of report automatically.)

The first staff member to schedule is Project Manager Bill Mata who has only one task. (See fig. 7.5.)

Assign your next resource, Bob Hancock, first to "Needs Analysis." (See fig. 7.6.) When he finishes this task, look down the next column of the Project Gantt Chart to see what jobs are available. Two jobs begin shortly after the end of his task: "Select Server" and "Select Software." There are three possible scenarios:

1. Bob has the skills to perform either task. Schedule other team members whose skills may be more limited first, then give Bob whatever is left over.

2. Bob has the skill to perform one of these tasks but not the other. Assign him the one he has the skill to perform.

3. Bob doesn't have the skill to perform any of the tasks that begin that week. This doesn't mean he isn't necessarily a valuable member of the team; sometimes work and skill just don't match up. Notice that Bob now becomes a *slack resource* (a resource without scheduled work for that period) until you are able to match him with a task for which he is skilled. You now have another week in which your resource need exceeds your available staff. As you did before, you will either have to adjust staff to meet the schedule (others work overtime or obtain another temporary staff member) or have to adjust the schedule to meet the staff (rearrange tasks to bring forward something Bob can do, or push everything back and possibly delay the project completion).

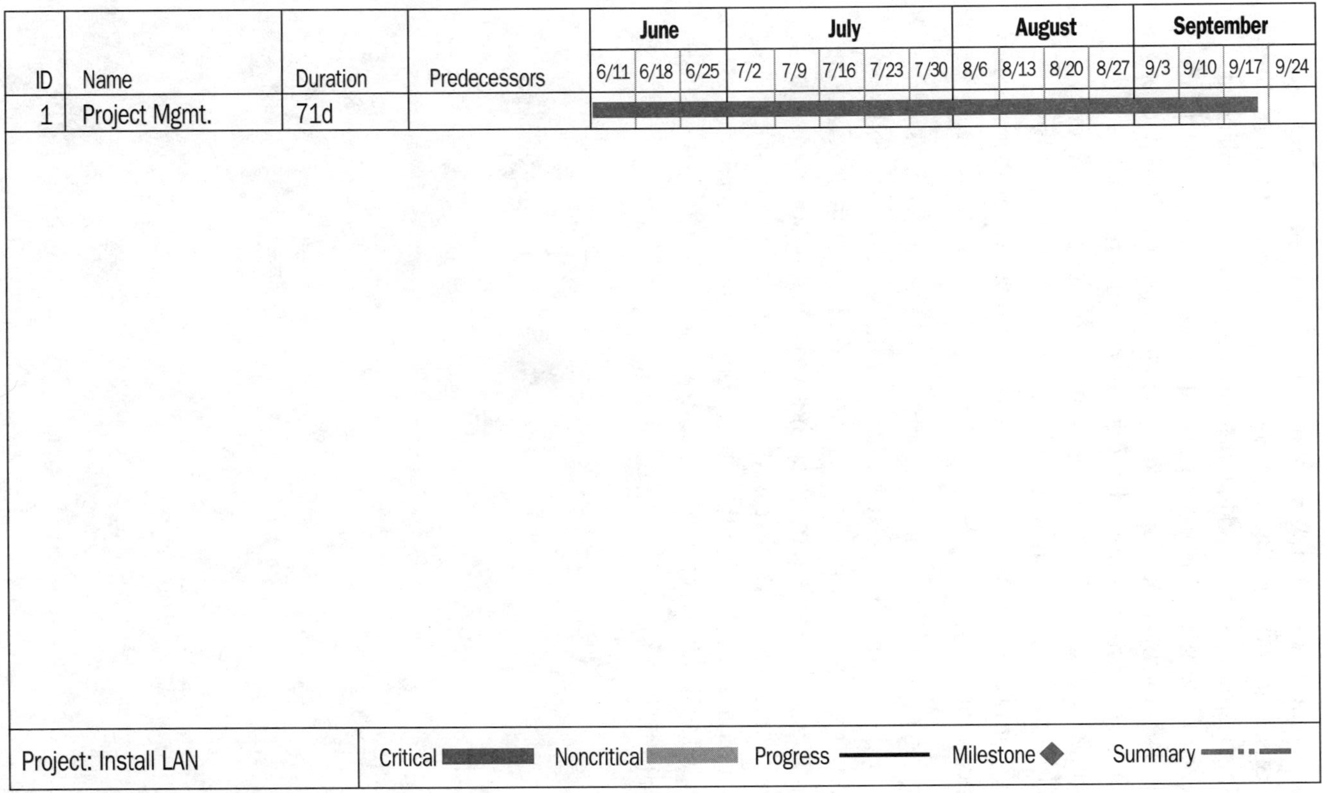

ID	Name	Duration	Predecessors	June			July				August				September			
				6/11	6/18	6/25	7/2	7/9	7/16	7/23	7/30	8/6	8/13	8/20	8/27	9/3	9/10	9/17	9/24
1	Project Mgmt.	71d																	

Project: Install LAN

Critical ▬▬ Noncritical ▬▬ Progress ▬▬ Milestone ◆ Summary ▬■■▬

Fig. 7.5. Resource Gantt Chart for Bill Mata.

Let's assume Bob does have the necessary skills. You assign all his tasks, but find out that there's nothing else for him to do after he finishes training users. He's now a "slack resource." Slack at the end of the project is not as useful as slack during a project, but it does mean he is available for crash support at the end of the project. Since you don't have as much margin in your schedule as you ideally wanted, he may be a good emergency resource for later. Perhaps he can help with the end of "Test/Debug" and "Acceptance." Or, he can be released early, lowering project salary costs.

Now, assign work to your temporary employee, Claudia (see fig. 7.7). Inspect the Project Gantt Chart for the overload period, looking for tasks that fit together, both in terms of their schedule location and the skills required. The two construction-trade jobs, "Wire Office" and "Connect Network" seem like good back-to-back possibilities. (Notice that these jobs require specialized skills, so you must recruit a temporary resource with those skills.) Assign those to Claudia Geary.

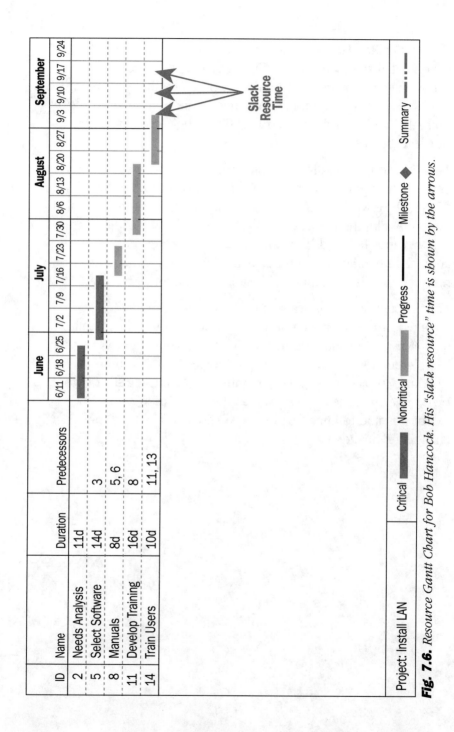

ID	Name	Duration	Predecessors	June			July			August			September		
				6/11	6/18	6/25	7/2	7/9	7/16	7/23	7/30	8/6	8/13	8/20	8/27	9/3	9/10	9/17	9/24
2	Needs Analysis	11d																	
5	Select Software	14d	3																
8	Manuals	8d	5, 6																
11	Develop Training	16d	8																
14	Train Users	10d	11, 13																

Slack
Resource
Time

Project: Install LAN   Critical ▬▬ Noncritical ▬▬ Progress ▬▬ Milestone ◆ Summary ▬▬▬

Fig. 7.6. *Resource Gantt Chart for Bob Hancock. His "slack resource" time is shown by the arrows.*

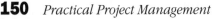

That leaves Rey Harter. Assign his work as you did Bob's, looking for potential skill and task conflicts. Assume you don't find any. Unfortunately, you do find a different problem: there are no tasks available for him to perform from the middle of the week of 8/6 to the beginning of the week of 8/20 (see fig. 7.8). Rey is now a "slack resource" for that period.

This situation is actually desirable, because Rey can serve as emergency support for any problems that occur during the "Connect Network" and "Develop Training" tasks assigned to that period. Again, the presence of slack resource time lowers project risk, because Rey and Bob can be shifted to speed up key project tasks or to handle emergencies as they crop up. Although slack resource time is not infinitely flexible, it's still an asset.

(Tip! Though it sometimes seems sensible to schedule less qualified or productive employees as slack resources, remember that your slack resources are also your emergency reserve. More flexible employees may be a better choice. Also, if you are a "working" project manager—you must do technical tasks on your own projects—schedule yourself as the slack resource to the extent possible to improve your flexibility and ability to meet changing demands.)

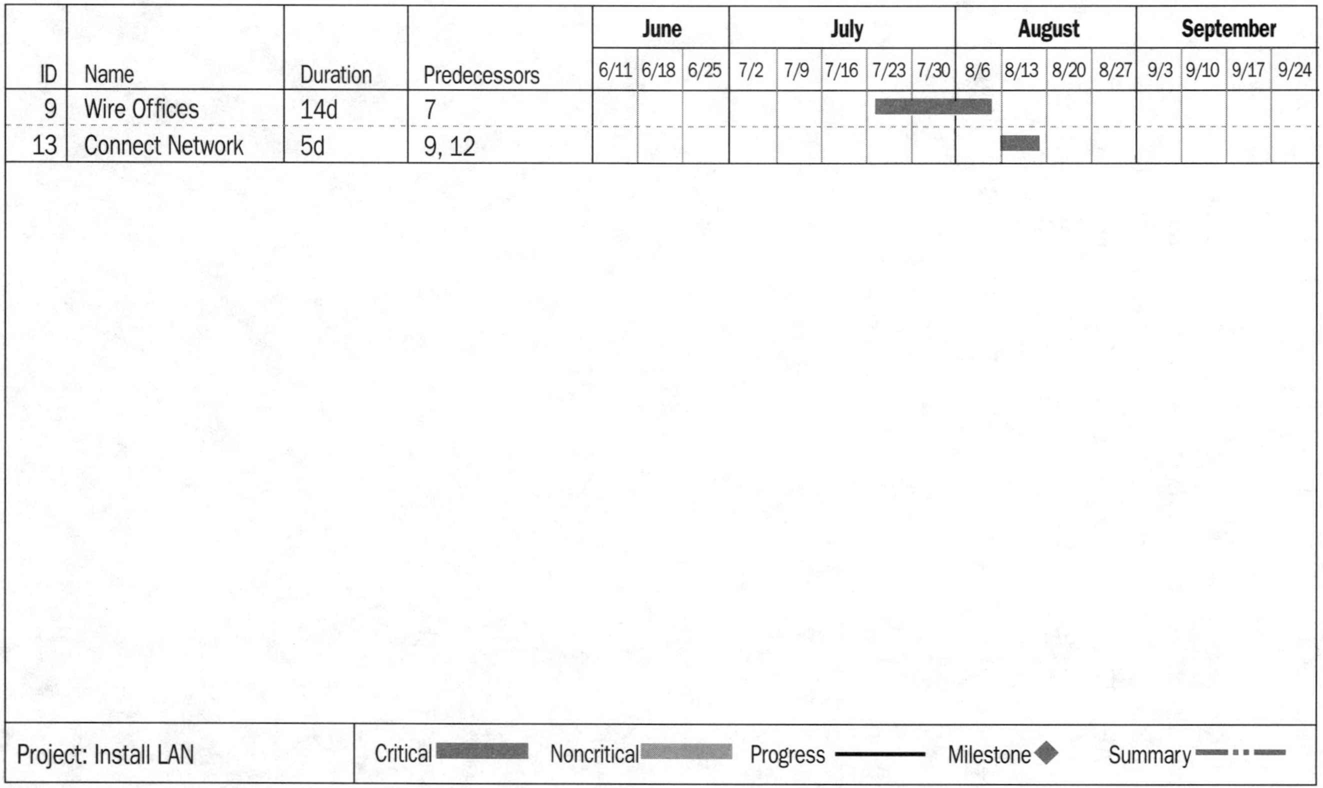

ID	Name	Duration	Predecessors	June 6/11	6/18	6/25	7/2	July 7/9	7/16	7/23	7/30	8/6	August 8/13	8/20	8/27	9/3	September 9/10	9/17	9/24
9	Wire Offices	14d	7																
13	Connect Network	5d	9, 12																

Project: Install LAN   Critical ▬   Noncritical ▬   Progress ▬   Milestone ◆   Summary ▬▬▬

Fig. 7.7. *Resource Gantt Chart for Claudia Geary.*

With more complicated scheduling situations, the procedure is the same.

Tip! For very large projects with hundreds of staff members, first schedule the project using generic job titles and quantities, not individual people (e.g., "Programmer x 6," "Technician x 3," "Carpenter x 12," "Industrial Engineer x 2"). If you're using software (and for that size project you probably are), you can have it total up the number of person-hours for each occupation and derive your ideal project team size by using simple division.

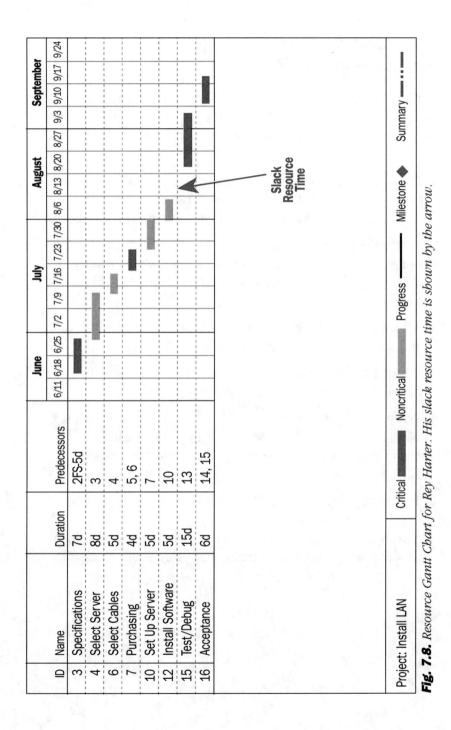

Fig. 7.8. *Resource Gantt Chart for Rey Harter. His slack resource time is shown by the arrow.*

Gantt Chart—Don't Manage Your Project Without It

Because the Gantt Chart is such a traditional tool and appears so simple on the surface, it doesn't always get the respect it deserves as a project management tool. Here are some of the uses of a Gantt Chart:

1. **Management reports.** The simplicity and visual strength of a Gantt Chart makes it the ideal tool to use when you're reporting to someone who doesn't know project management.

2. **Testing the Time constraint.** When you're doing preliminary project planning and have numerous parallel tasks, you often don't know how long the project will take in calendar time. The Gantt Chart will show you.

3. **Allocating resources.** The Gantt Chart helps you to allocate and track resources and identify conflicts.

4. **What-If analysis.** You can explore many options visually and determine which one(s) are best for your project.

5. **Resource management.** The "Resource Gantt Chart" works both in controlling resources on a single project and in managing resources across projects in a multiple project environment.

6. **Tracking progress.** The "Tracking Gantt Chart," which you'll explore later, allows you to compare actual project performance to plan, shows you the consequence of tasks not finishing on their assigned times, and gives you a tool to explore options.

Create Your Own Gantt Chart

Create a Gantt Chart from the following Task Table.

Task Table		
Task	**Duration**	**Dependency**
A	2	N/A
B	1	A
C	2	A
D	1	B, C
E	2	D
F	1	D
G	1	E, F

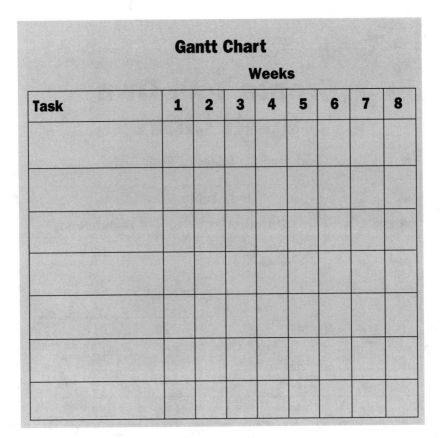

Answer Key for Exercise #8

Gantt Chart

Weeks

Task	1	2	3	4	5	6	7	8
A	▬	▬						
B			▬					
C			▬	▬				
D					▬			
E						▬	▬	
F						▬		
G								▬

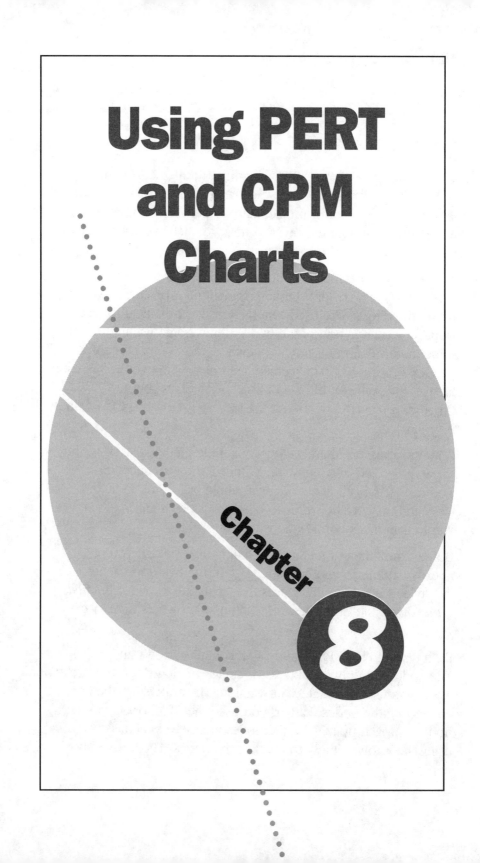

Using PERT and CPM Charts

Chapter 8

How to Create a PERT/CPM Chart

You've already explored PERT charting as a method of creating your initial project dependency sequence. Now, let's delve further into this powerful set of project management tools to discover more options and more power to help you achieve your goal: on time, on budget, and to performance standards.

As mentioned previously, although PERT and CPM are two different systems for project management, in a practical, everyday sense, these terms are used synonymously. Virtually all project managers use a hybrid of the two systems. Some use more PERT, some more CPM, but a mix nonetheless. Most computer software packages for project management also blend the two. In Microsoft Project, for example, the menu lists "PERT Chart" but not "CPM Chart" as a display option, but the display is closer to CPM than it is to PERT.

Both PERT and CPM are *network* planning methods. That is, they show the project as a network of linked and sequenced tasks. You can analyze the network as a whole or just the individual tasks and their relationships to other tasks. Such analyses allow you to gain insight and options for your project.

Besides the different methods of telling time (which you've already explored), another difference in the two approaches is the style of charting. PERT uses the technique known as *activity on arrow*, while CPM uses the technique known as *activity on node*.

Each type of chart, PERT and CPM, contains arrows and nodes. The nodes are drawn as boxes or circles, analogous to the Sticky Notes you used to create your version. The arrows are the lines connecting the nodes. Earlier, you used the CPM, or activity on node approach by making the nodes themselves the tasks, and using the arrows simply to connect the nodes. The arrows show dependencies.

Activity on node charting is used as the primary tool in this book for three reasons:

1. It allows you to use Sticky Note PERT, working directly from the WBS to an initial project layout.

2. The majority of project management software packages use this approach, meaning that you're more likely to encounter it.

3. It avoids the "dummy arrow" issue, which is necessary in activity on arrow charting (see sidebar on page 166).

On the other hand, it loses one advantage of the activity on arrow charting technique: You can't draw it easily to timescale.

Using tasks from the sample LAN installation project, let's show various relationships in activity on node charting.

Referring to figure 8.1, you'll notice that "Select Cables" is dependent on "Select Server."

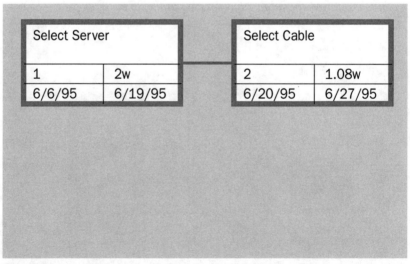

Fig. 8.1. *Activity on node charting for sample LAN installation project. "Select Cables" is dependent on "Select Server."*

Figure 8.2 shows that "Select Software" and "Select Server" are both dependent on "Specifications." They are parallel to one another.

Specifications		Select Software	
1	1.5w	3	3w
6/6/95	6/15/95	6/15/95	7/6/95

Select Server	
2	2w
6/15/95	6/29/95

Fig. 8.2. *Both the "Select Software" task and the "Select Server" task are dependent on "Specifications," but they're parallel to each other.*

In figure 8.3 you can see that "Purchasing" is dependent on both "Select Software" and "Select Cables." They are parallel to one another.

Select Software		Purchasing	
1	3w	3	0.92w
6/6/95	6/26/95	6/27/95	7/3/95

Select Cables	
2	1.08w
6/6/95	6/13/95

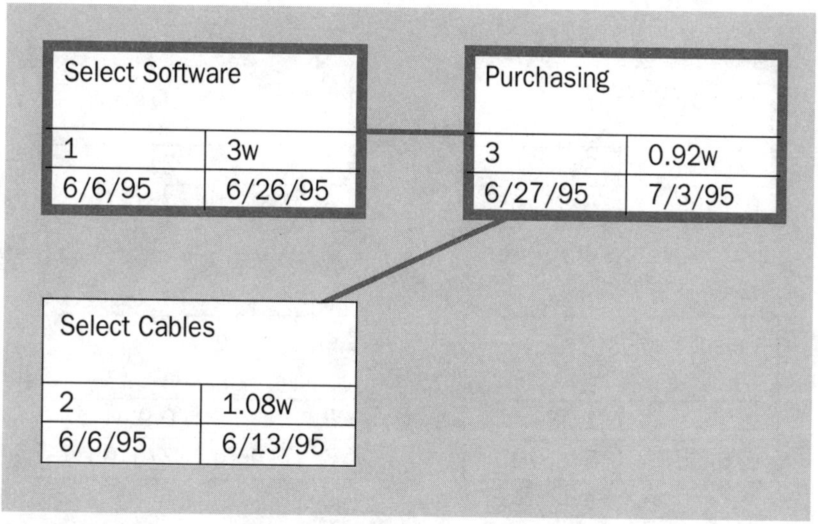

Fig. 8.3. *Activity on node charting for sample LAN installation project. "Purchasing" is dependent on both "Select Software" and "Select Cables." They are parallel to one another.*

"Manuals" and "Purchasing" are both dependent on both "Select Software" and "Select Cables," as shown in figure 8.4. Both pairs are parallel to one another.

Select Software		
1	3w	
6/6/95	6/26/95	

Manuals		
4	3w	
6/27/95	7/17/95	

Select Cables		
2	1.08w	
6/6/95	6/13/95	

Purchasing		
3	0.92w	
6/27/95	7/3/95	

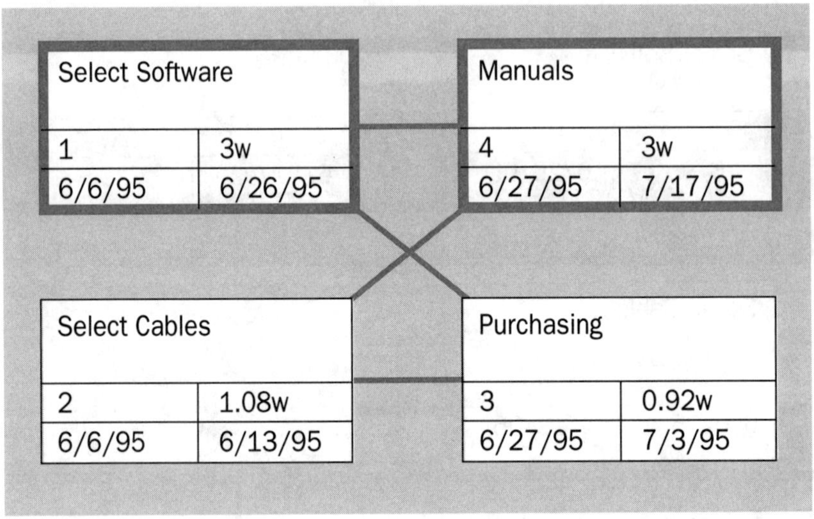

Fig. 8.4. *Both "Manuals" and "Purchasing" are dependent on two tasks: "Select Software" and "Select Cables." Further, both sets of tasks are parallel to one another.*

As shown in figure 8.5, "Test/Debug" is dependent upon "Connect Network." "Train Users," however, is dependent on both "Connect Network" and "Develop Training. "Connect Network" and "Develop Training" are parallel; "Test/Debug" and "Train Users" are parallel although they aren't directly related.

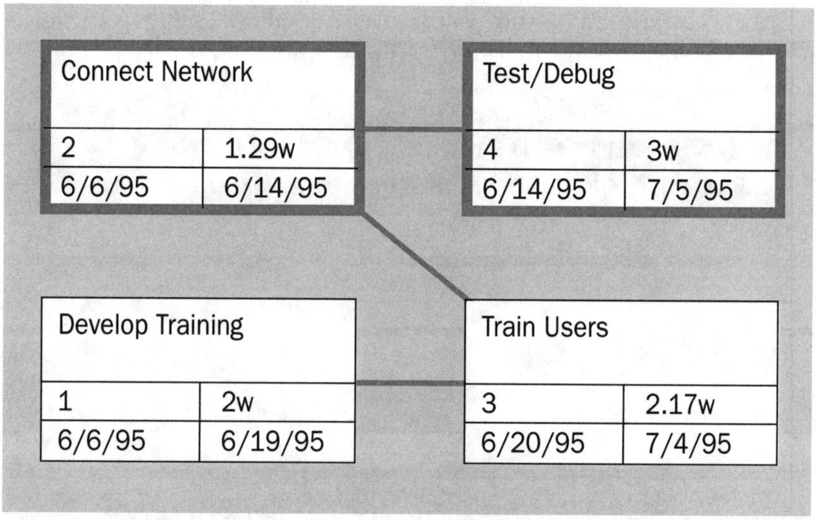

Connect Network		Test/Debug	
2	1.29w	4	3w
6/6/95	6/14/95	6/14/95	7/5/95

Develop Training		Train Users	
1	2w	3	2.17w
6/6/95	6/19/95	6/20/95	7/4/95

Fig. 8.5. *In this phase, "Test/Debug" and "Train Users" are dependent on "Connect Network." There are two sets of parallel tasks: "Connect Network" and "Develop Training," and "Test/Debug" and "Train Users."*

Activity on Arrow Charting

If you're curious about "activity on arrow" as an alternate charting approach, here's an overview.

In this technique (actually PERT in the strict sense), the arrows are the tasks and the nodes are called "events": they show the beginning and end of tasks and serve as short-term checkpoints.

As figures 8.6a to 8.7b show, you can show the same relationships using the activity on arrow method as you did with activity on node.

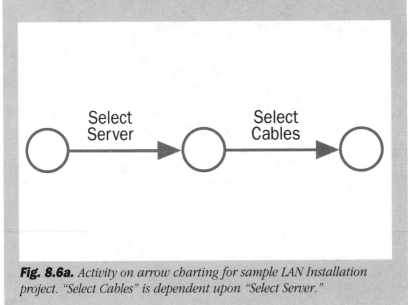

Fig. 8.6a. *Activity on arrow charting for sample LAN Installation project. "Select Cables" is dependent upon "Select Server."*

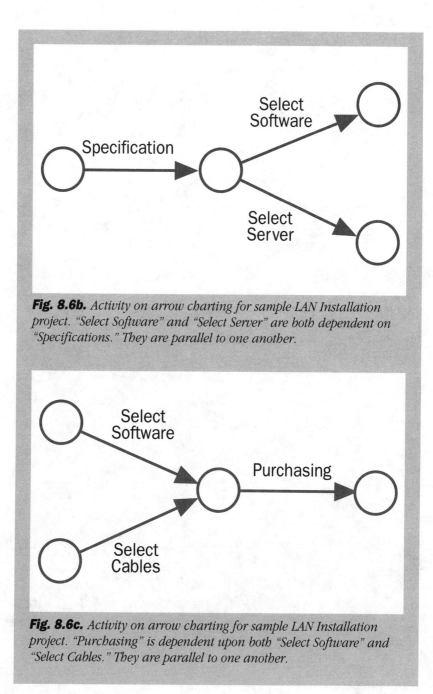

Fig. 8.6b. *Activity on arrow charting for sample LAN Installation project. "Select Software" and "Select Server" are both dependent on "Specifications." They are parallel to one another.*

Fig. 8.6c. *Activity on arrow charting for sample LAN Installation project. "Purchasing" is dependent upon both "Select Software" and "Select Cables." They are parallel to one another.*

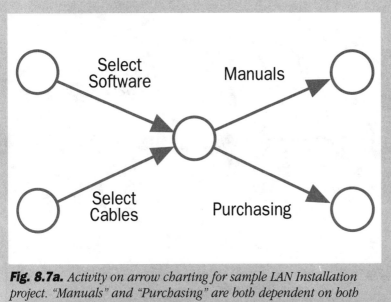

Fig. 8.7a. *Activity on arrow charting for sample LAN Installation project. "Manuals" and "Purchasing" are both dependent on both "Select Software" and "Select Cables." Both pairs are parallel to one another.*

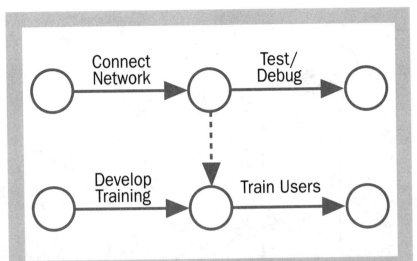

Fig. 8.7b. *Activity on arrow charting for sample LAN Installation project. "Test/Debug" is dependent upon "Connect Network." "Train Users," however, is dependent on both "Connect Network" and "Develop Training. "Connect Network" and "Develop Training" are parallel; "Test/Debug" and "Train Users" are parallel although they are not directly related.*

The dotted arrow, called a *dummy task,* shows a dependency relationship where there is no actual task to connect the nodes. This is necessary in "activity on arrow" charting, but not in "activity on node" charting.

Earlier, the reasons why "activity on node" charting is preferred in this book were listed. There is one deficiency in this choice: because the arrows can be drawn to any desired length, you can make a timeline with the "activity on arrow" technique, allowing you to combine advantages of both PERT and Gantt in the same chart (see fig 8.8).

Figure 8.9 shows the entire project network charted in activity on node.

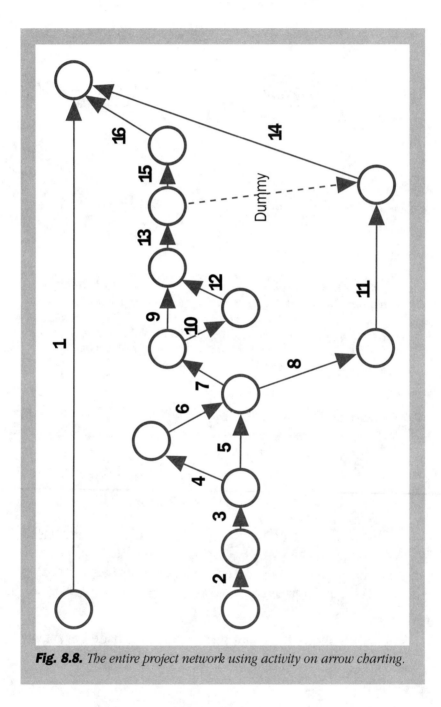

Fig. 8.8. *The entire project network using activity on arrow charting.*

Determining the Critical Path, Critical Tasks, and Slack

As with a Gantt Chart, the important thing about CPM and PERT charting is how to use it to gain insight into your project.

The following key concepts and technical terms are necessary for you to know to analyze PERT/CPM charts.

Paths

A *path* is a sequence of tasks in a dependent order. A *full path* is a sequence that leads from the first task of a project to the final path of the project. A *path segment* is a sequence of tasks in between two tasks that are inside the project; that is, not including both the first and the last task.

The length of a full path or a path segment is the sum of the times of the tasks on that path.

The *Critical Path* is the longest full path in a project. You may have multiple critical paths if more than one path is tied in length for the longest path.

Tasks

A *critical task* is a task on the critical path.

A *noncritical task* is a task on any path or path segment that isn't critical.

Slack

Slack and *float* are synonyms (this book uses "slack") that refer to the extra time available to perform noncritical tasks. Slack comes in two varieties: total slack and free slack. *Total slack* is the amount of time a task can be delayed without delaying the end of the project. *Free slack* is the amount of time a task can be delayed without delaying the start of the next task.

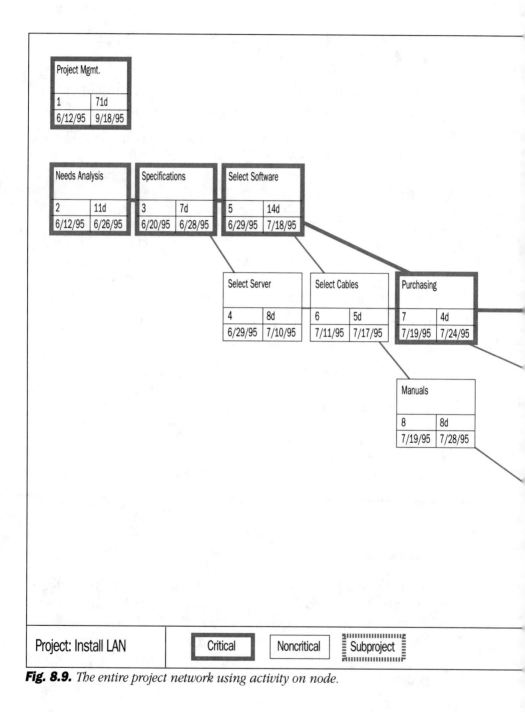

Fig. 8.9. *The entire project network using activity on node.*

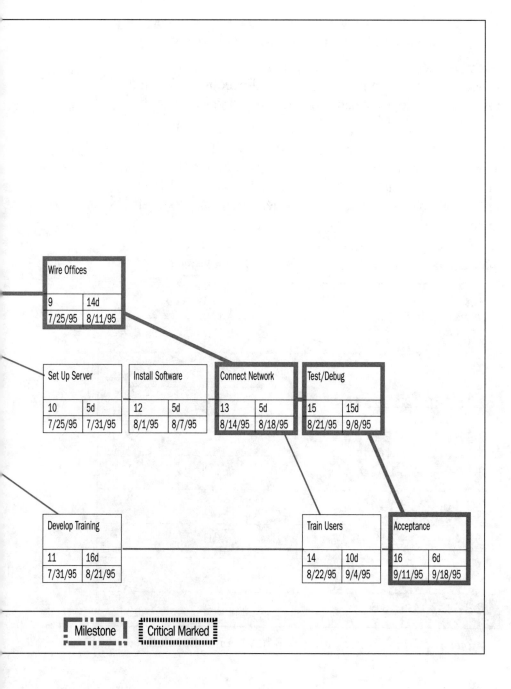

Wire Offices	
9	14d
7/25/95	8/11/95

Set Up Server	
10	5d
7/25/95	7/31/95

Install Software	
12	5d
8/1/95	8/7/95

Connect Network	
13	5d
8/14/95	8/18/95

Test/Debug	
15	15d
8/21/95	9/8/95

Develop Training	
11	16d
7/31/95	8/21/95

Train Users	
14	10d
8/22/95	9/4/95

Acceptance	
16	6d
9/11/95	9/18/95

Milestone   Critical Marked

Negative slack refers to a situation in which there isn't enough time (a negative amount of time) to accomplish a task.

Several of these steps are done automatically by project management software packages. You still need to understand how these are done by hand so that you will know what the computer is up to.

As noted, a path is a sequence of tasks. Just follow the connecting lines from task to task, starting with the first task in the project and following on to the end. For the sample LAN installation project, several full paths lead from start to finish (see Table 8.1).

Table 8.1 **Full Paths for Sample LAN Installation Project**

Path	Times
2-3-5-7-9-13-15-16	71
2-3-5-7-9-13-14-16	66
2-3-5-7-10-12-13-15-16	67
2-3-5-7-10-12-13-14-16	62
2-3-4-6-7-9-13-15-16	69
2-3-4-6-7-9-13-14-16	64
2-3-4-6-7-10-12-13-15-16	66
2-3-4-6-7-10-12-13-14-16	61
2-3-4-6-8-11-14-16	64

(*Note:* The 5-day overlap in Task 3 has been subtracted.)

The longest path, or the Critical Path, is 2-3-5-7-9-13-15-16, requiring a total of 71 days. Remember, by definition, the Critical Path is the length of time the project is expected to take. (Notice that the "1" path, consisting only of Task 1, is also 71 days, but that path isn't considered "critical" because it refers only to the project manager. Remember, there's disagreement about whether this task should be included in the project at all. Your role as project manager will take exactly as long as the full project takes, no matter what. Ignore a path consisting solely of the project manager in calculating Critical Path.)

Why have a special name for the longest path? Why not just call it "longest path"? Imagine that it takes longer to finish "Specifications" than the schedule permits. Notice the start of "Select Server" is automatically delayed, which bumps "Select Cables" and so on down the Critical Path, finally bumping "Acceptance." *When you make the longest (critical) path longer, the project automatically becomes longer.*

On the other hand, what if "Select Software" is late? The path segment between "Specifications" and "Purchasing" contains Tasks 4 and 6, with a total time of thirteen working days. "Select Software" takes fourteen days. Tasks 4 and 6 can be up to one day late without jeopardizing the start of "Purchasing. Therefore, Task 4 has a total slack (slack that won't endanger the end of the project) of one day, but no free slack (won't jeopardize the start of the next task). Task 6 has both total slack and free slack of one day, since a day late would jeopardize neither the end of the project nor the start of the next task. (Notice that another way to think of a critical task is that it has total slack and free slack of zero.)

Here's another example. Take a look at the path segment between "Purchasing" (Task 7) and "Connect Network" (Task 13). Task 9, a critical task, takes fourteen days. Task 10 and Task 12 together take ten days. Those two tasks each have total slack of four days (14 days on the Critical Path minus 10 days on the non-

Critical Path). Total slack belongs to both tasks, though if Task 10 is late, it robs slack from "Install Software." Task 10 has no free slack, because any lateness delays the start of Task 12. Task 12 has free slack of four days, since it can be that late without jeopardizing the start of Task 13.

The concepts of critical tasks and slack have profound implications for the management of your project. They tell you where to focus, help you manage your risk, and identify extra time and options for achieving your goals.

Critical Path Software Shortcut

You'll note that in figure 8.9, the Critical Path boxes have thicker borders and appear on top. If you'll look back at the earlier project Gantt Charts, you'll also find that the Critical Path tasks have darker bars than the noncritical tasks. Most project management software provides automatic Critical Path calculation.

The most efficient way to determine Critical Paths and slack is to do a *forward pass* and then a *backward pass* through your project.

In the forward pass, start with Task 1 and write down the earliest date that task can start (normally the end date of the predecessor task if you're using FS dependencies). This is called the *early start*. Do the same for each task from start to finish.

Then perform a backward pass. Starting with the final task and working backward, write down the last date a task can start without affecting its successor task. This is called the *late start*. Do the same for each task.

For each task, if the early start and late start dates are identical, the task is on the Critical Path. If there is a difference between the early start and late start dates, the difference is the available slack for that task.

Here is a table of early start and late start dates prepared by software for the sample LAN installation project. It shows available free slack and total slack in *elapsed days* (ed).

Table 8.2 Early Start and Late Start Dates for Sample LAN Installation Project

ID	Name	Scheduled Start	Scheduled Finish	Late Start	Scheduled Finish	Free Slack	Total Slack
1	Project Mgmt.	6/12/96 8:00 am	9/18/96 5:00 pm	6/12/96 8:00 am	9/18/96 5:00 pm	0ed	0ed
2	Needs Analysis	6/12/96 8:00 am	6/26/96 5:00 pm	6/12/96 8:00 am	6/26/96 5:00 pm	0ed	0ed
3	Specifications	6/20/96 8:00 am	6/28/96 5:00 pm	6/20/96 8:00 am	6/28/96 5:00 pm	0ed	0ed
4	Select Server	6/29/96 8:00 am	7/10/96 5:00 pm	6/30/96 8:00 am	7/11/96 5:00 pm	0.63ed	1ed
5	Select Software	6/29/96 8:00 am	7/18/96 5:00 pm	6/29/96 8:00 am	7/18/96 5:00 pm	0ed	0ed
6	Select Cables	7/11/96 8:00 am	7/17/96 5:00 pm	7/12/96 8:00 am	7/18/96 5:00 pm	1ed	1ed
7	Purchasing	7/19/96 8:00 am	7/24/96 5:00 pm	7/19/96 8:00 am	7/24/96 5:00 pm	0ed	0ed
8	Manuals	7/19/96 8:00 am	7/28/96 5:00 pm	7/25/96 8:00 am	8/3/96 5:00 pm	2.63ed	6ed
9	Wire Offices	7/25/96 8:00 am	8/11/96 5:00 pm	7/25/96 8:00 am	8/11/96 5:00 pm	0ed	0ed
10	Set Up Server	7/25/96 8:00 am	7/31/96 5:00 pm	7/31/96 8:00 am	8/4/96 5:00 pm	0.63ed	4ed
11	Develop Training	7/31/96 8:00 am	8/21/96 5:00 pm	8/4/96 8:00 am	8/25/96 5:00 pm	0.63ed	4ed
12	Install Software	8/1/96 8:00 am	8/7/96 5:00 pm	8/7/96 8:00 am	8/11/96 5:00 pm	4ed	4ed
13	Connect Network	8/14/96 8:00 am	8/18/96 5:00 pm	8/14/96 8:00 am	8/18/96 5:00 pm	0ed	0ed
14	Train Users	8/22/96 8:00 am	9/4/96 5:00 pm	8/28/96 8:00 am	9/8/96 5:00 pm	4ed	4ed
15	Test/Debug	8/21/96 8:00 am	9/8/96 5:00 pm	8/21/96 8:00 am	9/8/96 5:00 pm	0ed	0ed
16	Acceptance	9/11/96 8:00 am	9/18/96 5:00 pm	9/11/96 8:00 am	9/18/96 5:00 pm	0ed	0ed

How to Use the Critical Path for More Project Power

Conventional project management wisdom suggests that PERT/CPM techniques are used primarily for the control of large and complex projects. However, even if your projects are small, you can still use the power of the Critical Path to help you meet your project objectives. Here are several ways you can benefit:

Explore alternate ways to achieve your goal. Using Sticky Note PERT, you realized you could lay out a project several different ways, each offering options and tradeoffs of time, risk, and resources. If your project goal seems impossible, sometimes a different layout can make the impossible achievable.

Manage your time more effectively. As project manager, you're like the plate-spinning act on the old Ed Sullivan show, keeping multiple plates spinning at all times. You have to set priorities to survive. Critical tasks are necessarily of higher priority than noncritical tasks, because noncritical tasks can run late (up to their available slack) with no consequences for the project deadline.

Manage project risk. You learned previously that sigma (σ) is a measure of risk, and you can see the risk more clearly in your chart. Critical tasks with high σ values are the most dangerous to achieving your deadline. A noncritical task with slack $\geq 2\ \sigma$ has a 95 percent chance of meeting its deadline with no intervention or special action on your part. You can calculate σ for each path or path segment in your project, and identify potential problems.

When you identify problems of high σ and low (or no) slack, you can do any of the following:

- Redesign the workflow to put those tasks on paths with more slack.

- Add resources to lower risk.

- Give more management attention to those tasks.

- Redesign the task itself to lower its risk.

Move your resources where the problems are. As you'll recall, a slack resource is a resource on your team who does not have a current assignment. Perhaps there was no assignment available at that time. Perhaps the slack resource is performing a noncritical task and cannot be reassigned to new work until the path segment is finished. If the resource has the ability to help out elsewhere in the project, the resource may be assigned either in advance, as part of your planning, or held in reserve for emergencies.

For example, Task 6, "Select Cables," has one day of slack, both free and total. If you have assigned a full-time staff member to that task, that person has one day of slack in his or her schedule. If there is a problem with Task 5, "Select Software," which runs parallel and is on the Critical Path, the person can be selecting the software. That person has shifted for one day to get the work done with no consequence for the project deadline. If there is a problem in Task 6, that person can be up to one day behind schedule with no consequence for the project deadline. As you can see, slack lowers risk.

Adjust task start and finish dates to meet your needs. Holding some slack in reserve for emergencies is good project management strategy. Another option is to schedule some tasks for late start rather than early start. For example, you could start "Install Software" on 8/2/96, or deliberately choose to have it start on 8/3/96, if that would improve project flexibility or solve problems elsewhere on your project. Of course, it does lower the slack at the end of the task, giving you less margin should something go wrong in "Install Software."

Shorten your project. The power of CPM crash time becomes more readily apparent once you understand the concept of the Critical Path. Applying crash resources to Critical Path tasks shortens your total project time.

Warning! Check to see if changing your project times has created a new Critical Path. If you shorten a Critical Path segment by a greater amount than the slack available on its noncritical twin, all you do is switch which one is critical. Now, the old Critical Path is noncritical, with slack equal to the extra shortening.

Also, remember that crashing noncritical tasks is usually a waste of resources, since all you do is create more slack. There is an exception: if the noncritical task is very risky, and there is a significant likelihood that it will in fact exceed the available slack, then crashing that noncritical task may lower total project risk enough to be worthwhile.

Tip! If your project plan has lots of resource slack, try transferring people, equipment, and other resources from noncritical to critical tasks to get the benefit of crash time without spending extra money. Of course, keep checking to make sure you don't inadvertently change the Critical Path. There isn't anything wrong with changing the Critical Path if it seems smart to you, but it's dangerous for the Critical Path to change without you being aware of it.

Lower your costs. You can "reverse crash" noncritical tasks to save money. In CPM crash time, you spent resources to save time, but this is generally smart only on the Critical Path. Try to reverse this on noncritical tasks with lots of slack. Consider:

1. What is the cheapest you could accomplish the task, given unlimited time?

2. How much time would you have to spend? (Is there enough slack to cover the extra time?)

3. Calculate the crash slope for time spent and money saved. Is it worth it? If you're using free resources from slack paths, the answer is probably "yes." If the choice would make your project late, it may be worthwhile if budget is more important than the extra time.

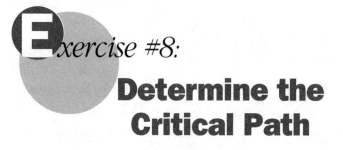

xercise #8:

Determine the Critical Path

Using the chart below, answer Questions 1 to 3 regarding Critical Path.

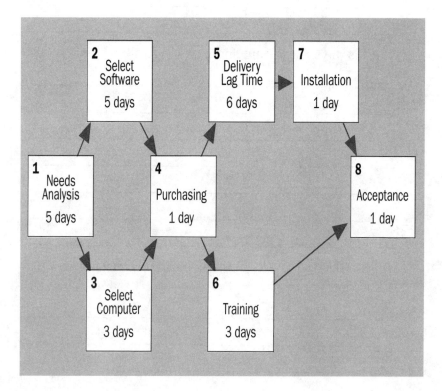

1. List the paths through this project shown on the previous page, and give the total time for each path.

_____

_____

_____

_____

_____

_____

2. Which is the Critical Path, and how long will this project take?

_____

_____

_____

_____

_____

_____

3. Which tasks have slack, and how much total slack does each task have?

_____

_____

_____

_____

_____

_____

_____

Answer Key for Exercise #9

1. Paths:

1-2-4-5-7-8	19 days
1-2-4-6-8	15 days
1-3-4-5-7-8	17 days
1-3-4-6-8	13 days

2. 1-2-4-5-7-8 is critical (it's the longest). Total project time is therefore 19 days.

3. Tasks 3 and 6 are the only two tasks not on the Critical Path. By comparing the shorter path segment to the longer path, you get the following slack results:

    Task 3: 2 days slack (Task 2 minus Task 3)

    Task 6: 4 days slack (Tasks 5 and 7 are both between 4 and 8; compare both to Task 6, giving 7 days minus 4 days.)

Budgeting for Projects

Chapter

9

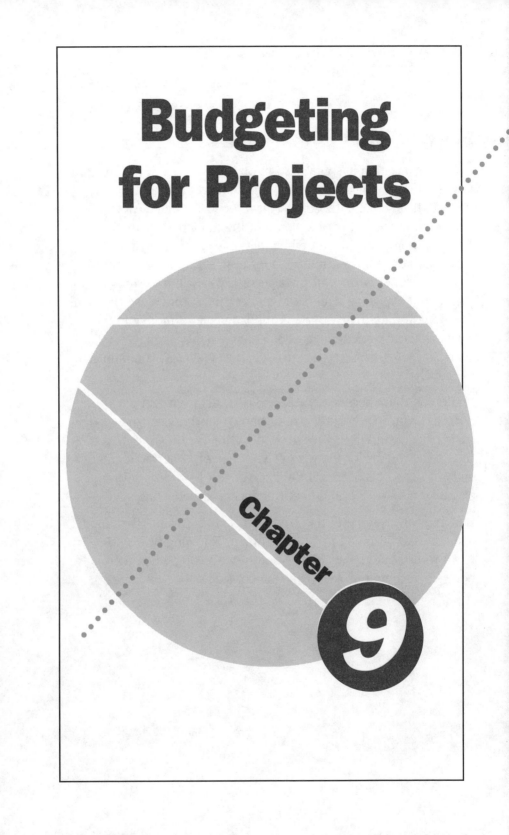

Finance for Project Managers

Every organization has its variation on the concept of the "hidden keys to the executive suite." It refers to the rules, explicit or implicit, that separate those who have or will achieve executive rank from those who won't. Some of the hidden keys are arbitrary. Some aren't. And while the keys of every organization vary, one key is universal: no matter how strong your technical skills, no matter what your track record, you will never be considered executive material in any organization unless and until you demonstrate that you speak the language of money in the terms financial professionals use. Finance is the language of senior management; if you don't speak it, you can't communicate effectively.

While you don't necessarily need to rush right out and get your MBA in finance (not that it would hurt), you do need to have a basic background in finance and budgeting for the sake of your project, as well as for the sake of your career. (The Bibliography and Suggested Resources at the back of this book lists several excellent books for honing your finance and budgeting skills.)

Budget is always one of the Triple Constraints. Even when budget is the weak constraint, it's still important. Knowing how and when to use budget flexibility—and how to cope when there is none—is a central project management skill.

Understanding Your Organization's Financial System

The first step in any organization is to make sure you understand your internal financial systems. Always make a friend (or friendly acquaintance) in the finance/accounting department so you can have someone to ask about internal rules. Here are five key questions to consider as you begin any project:

1. Have I accounted for both fixed and variable costs?

Fixed costs have a definite price. The server, cables, and software themselves are fixed costs. Variable costs change based on external factors. For example, labor is a variable cost, because it varies based on the amount of time it takes to install the software, run the wires, and so on.

Always estimate time first, and then budget, even when budget is the driver. Because labor costs money (unless you're running a volunteer staff—and even then you have overhead-type costs that vary by time), you must have your time estimates done in order to cost the project in the first place.

One bonus of the PERT time method you've learned in this book is that the same process that adjusts your time estimate also adjusts your estimates for the variable costs—giving you proportionally the same budget margin as you have time margin.

2. Are direct labor costs charged to my project budget, or am I charged only "hard" costs (equipment, rentals, outside contracts)?

If you aren't charged for direct labor, then direct labor is cheaper for you (even if it isn't necessarily a bargain for the organization as a whole). When faced with a choice between internal and external resources, use internal ones to reduce demand on your budget. If you're charged for direct labor costs, make sure you build them into your budget.

3. *Is my project charged for overhead, general and administrative (G&A), profit, or other burdens?*

In a comprehensive cost accounting system, certain organizational costs are allocated among the departments and projects. These include overhead (employee benefits, etc.), G&A (rent, utilities, support services), and built-in *profit targets* (the goal for how much profit the organization wants to earn on your project). These are normally quantified as percentages.

For example, you might have a G&A burden of 20 percent. That means 20 percent of your project budget is automatically spent to buy your share of the rent and utilities. You must deduct that money off the top. If employee benefits cost about one-third of direct labor costs, then you need to take your labor costs and add 33.3 percent to them. Overhead and profit targets are treated the same way as G&A burdens— direct charge to your project budget and taken off the top. (Overhead and profit are normally billed on contract jobs, and are less frequently charged on internal projects.)

You can easily have a situation in which 40 percent to 50 percent of your ostensible project budget is not available for direct project expenses! This isn't necessarily a recipe for disaster, unless you get caught unaware. When planning your budget or asking for the desired funding, make sure you account for these hidden costs and put them upfront in your proposal.

4. *Will my project time span coincide with key financial cycle dates, and how will those affect me?*

Many organizations have some seasonality in money. For example, the deadline in the sample LAN installation project is influenced by the upcoming end of the fiscal year, which impacts the availability of funds. If you're a government contractor, the government fiscal year cycle can wreak havoc on your schedule. Certain retail businesses (the toy business, for example) are highly dependent on the Christmas buying season for most of their revenue—they are cash-rich in January, cash-poor in September.

If you don't know about seasonality and financial cycle issues in your organization, use that friend in finance. You must have this information in a form specific to your organization. If you switch companies, don't assume the rules you learned still apply. Each organization has its unique issues. Learn them.

5. *If I'm doing a project for an outside client or customer, what accounting and financial issues do they have?*

Ask the same questions for your client or customer as you would for an internal client. Make sure you know about any special issues the client has that can affect your project.

Identifying Key Project Financial Issues

Besides overall organizational financial issues, you may have a number of financial and budget problems unique to your particular project.

1. *Do other departments within my organization have to perform portions of this project? Must I account for their costs? How do I get good estimates from them?*

The problem of support group estimates is sometimes substantial. This occurs when you must add to your budget the costs that someone not under your control will incur. For example, in the sample LAN project, you might ask the building maintenance staff to string the LAN wires in the walls. This is additional work for them—it's not accounted for in their budget. They want your budget to pay their costs, which is reasonable. The question is, how much should you allow? Negotiate this upfront, and be aware of a tendency for others to inflate their estimates to lower their risk at the expense of your project budget (or to free up some of their money for other unrelated work).

2. *Am I making my labor cost estimates based on getting specific people, or on more general standards?*

The "person-month" problem occurs when you create a time estimate for a task based on the idea that you will get Suzy Superstar instead of Tom Turkey as a member of your project team. If you build the estimate around Suzy's superior performance and you get Tom, your project estimates fly right out the window. Either make sure you get Suzy in the first place or make the time estimate based on an average performer. This problem also occurs if you base all your time estimates on your personal skill level and you are more experienced than your associates and team members are.

Tip! You could make Suzy's estimate $T(o)$, Tom's $T(p)$, and someone who is average in skill $T(m)$, and then calculate $T(e)$ for your project estimate.

3. *Will my project either take years to complete and/or involve international operations?*

Although at the time of this writing, inflation isn't the immediate threat it once was, even low inflation over a long enough period of time can drive up project costs substantially. Build in an inflation allowance on multiyear projects.

A bigger danger is currency exchange rate fluctuations on international projects. You need to build in an allowance, which you can base on historical data, worst-case scenario, or the best you can get away with.

4. Is my project heavily research and development (R&D) oriented, making many of my budget issues essentially unpredictable?

When you explored the difficulties of putting a man on the moon in Chapter 2, one part of the difficulty was putting together a valid budget estimate in the first place. On the surface, this was an impossible task, because even for the head of NASA, there were so many utterly unknown variables that an accurate estimate couldn't be achieved. How can you put together a reasonable estimate under these circumstances? Depending on the related or similar project experiences you've had or can discover, you may use any of the following estimating techniques:

Order of Magnitude Analysis (±35% accuracy). At the time of the NASA project, the U.S. had never gone to the moon, but had launched Vanguard. This is considered a "related" experience. From this, you can estimate an "order of magnitude" factor, which is how many times more difficult going to the moon is versus launching the Vanguard satellite. Multiply the Vanguard budget times the order of magnitude factor, and you have an estimate that is ±35 percent accurate—and that may be the best you can achieve. Make sure you explain this to your client/customer/boss/project originator, and document your explanation.

Approximate Estimate (±15% accuracy). The only difference between this method and Order of Magnitude Analysis is the quality of the comparable experience, which is "similar" rather than "related." That is to say it's closer to the current situation than "related." Vanguard was only *related* to Mercury, but Apollo was *similar* to Mercury and Gemini. Again, multiply the actual budget of the similar experience times an order of magnitude factor. Because the comparable experience is closer, the accuracy of the estimate is better: ±15 percent.

Detailed Cost Data (±5-7% accuracy). Here, you break down the project into its tasks and cost each element in detail. This is the most time-consuming but the most accurate of the methods. There is still a variance of 5 to 7 percent because no two situations are ever exactly alike.

Learning Curves Method. "Practice makes perfect—or at least better." Both Apollo 11 and Apollo 12 went to the moon. They were nearly identical in mission structure. Should the cost estimate have been the same for each? The Learning Curves Method says that subsequent repetitions should cost less because you learn from each experience. The first Saturn V booster rocket cost more than the next, and so forth. If two projects are identical in structure, lessons learned from the first should make the second cheaper.

General SWAG. Get a dart board and make a guess. Give it your best shot—sometimes that's all you have to go on. The accuracy of this method depends on the quality of your experience and judgment. Figure it as "± your job."

Job Costing the Project

There is yet another method of project estimating: your client/customer/boss tells you how much you have to spend and your job is to make it all fit. There may really be only that amount of money. Or, there are other demands on the money. Or, there may be room to negotiate. If you plan to negotiate your project budget, keep these two essentials in mind as you plan your strategy:

1. The earlier you start the negotiation, the more options are usually available.

2. If it all comes down to your guess versus your boss's guess, your boss wins. Rank hath its privilege. To trump your boss's opinion, you need facts. Hard data. Do your homework before you negotiate.

Now go through the process of fitting a project into an existing and fixed budget. Assume you're given a budget of $40,000 to install the LAN system. Can you do it?

You can try. First, for help in resource costing, check the features of your project management software. Most full-featured programs allow you not only to assign resources to jobs, but also to enter the cost of using those resources (e.g., salaries, overtime rates, etc.) and then to create budget reports using that data. Figure 9.1 was produced using a conventional spreadsheet program.

Using the time estimates and staff assignments from your previous work, you can cost the direct labor. The benefits and overhead columns are straight percentage multipliers. Contracts, materials, and supplies are described on the worksheet (see fig. 9.1).

Task	Days	Labor	Overhead	Contracts	Materials	Supplies	G&A	TOTAL
1. Project Mgmt.	71	$11,360	$3,749	$0	$0	$0	$1,511	$16,620
2. Needs Analysis	11	1,056	348	0	0	0	140	1,545
3. Specifications	7	672	222	0	0	0	89	983
4. Select Server	8	768	253	0	0	0	102	1,124
5. Select Software	14	1,344	444	0	0	0	179	1,966
6. Select Cables	5	480	158	0	0	0	64	702
7. Purchasing	4	384	127	0	6,750	0	726	7,987
8. Manuals	8	768	253	0	0	0	102	1,124
9. Wire Offices	14	1,120	370	0	0	750	224	2,464
10. Set Up Server	5	480	158	0	0	0	64	702
11. Develop Training	16	1,536	507	1,000	0	0	304	3,347
12. Install Software	5	480	158	0	0	0	64	702
13. Connect Network	5	400	132	0	0	0	53	585
14. Train Users	10	960	317	3,000	0	500	478	5,254
15. Test/Debug	15	1,440	475	0	0	0	192	2,107
16. Acceptance	6	576	190	0	0	0	77	843
TOTALS	204	$23,824	$7,862	$4,000	$6,750	$1,250	$4,369	$48,055

Staff				Materials		Extra Charges
Project Manager	$20	per hour		Computer	$5,000	Overhead
Assigned to Task 1	$160	per day		Software	1,000	33%
				Cables	250	
Computer Analyst	$12	per hour	(2 on team)	Connectors	500	G&A
Assigned to remaining	$96	per day		TOTAL	$6,750	10%
Maintenance Staff	$10	per hour		**Contracts:**		
Assigned to Tasks 9, 13	$80	per day		Training		
				Development	$1,000	
				Train Users	3,000	

Fig. 9.1. Budget Worksheet for the Sample LAN Installation Project.

You'll notice immediately that the initial pass puts you more than $8,000 over budget—and that's before you even get started on the work! You may have also noticed something else: *if you weren't charged the benefits and overhead burdens, you'd be nearly $4,000 under budget!*

Although this can be frustrating, it shouldn't be surprising. Overhead and benefits are real organizational costs, and they must be accounted for. In a previous chapter, you were able to lower your time estimate for the project. Now let's see what you can do to lower budget projections.

One idea you used to save time won't work for money: making tasks parallel. While time can be paralleled, money can't be. Money doesn't care if it's on the Critical Path or not.

Here are several tools that do work to help create a workable final budget:

- **Eliminate nonessential elements.** Take a good look at each task. Does it need to be done at all? Does it need to be done the way you've designed?

- **Check crash time results.** Because certain costs go away when a project is shortened, sometimes crashing a given task can save more than it costs when the entire project is considered.

- **Do it a cheaper way.** Look at your specifications. Do you really need the high-priced spread, or will Brand X achieve the same results?

- **Move slack resources.** Use the "reverse crash" method to see if you can save money by using some of your slack.

- **Spend money that isn't budgeted to your project.** If you're charged for contracts but not for staff work, use staff work even if the real cost is higher, because that money isn't charged to your project.

- **Check constraint priority.** If budget is the weak constraint, you might not worry about being over.

- **Renegotiate.** Armed with solid evidence, you might renegotiate the budget and get more money.

Now that you're aware of these tools, return to your budget worksheet for the LAN Installation project (see fig. 9.1), and try the following ideas:

- **Shop for a cheaper computer.** Try a clone brand. Instead of buying all the computing horsepower you might need in the long run, buy an upgradeable machine of more limited capacity. Also, buy less robust software, allowing for a later upgrade. Don't compromise cables and connectors. Cut supplies for wiring by borrowing from other departments.

- **Put yourself as the project manager to work.** Personally do "Needs Analysis," "Purchasing," and "Acceptance," and half of "Test/Debug." This takes a big bite out of staff salaries. This project really doesn't need a full-time project manager. Still, assign yourself last so that you don't find yourself overburdened operationally. Your first role is to manage the project. (Note that assigning yourself to those tasks should speed up their completion, but don't put the time savings on your schedule just yet. Remember, you have less than 2 σ of margin, so this extra time is part of your defense against schedule slippage.)

- **Negotiate harder on the training costs (development and training itself).** Cut the training supplies budget with smaller manuals. Figure on providing followup and technical support no matter what.

By implementing these strategies, you now have a budget of less than $40,000! (See fig. 9.2.)

Task	Days	Labor	Overhead	Contracts	Materials	Supplies	G&A	TOTAL
1. Project Mgmt.	71	$11,360	$3,749	$0	$0	$0	$1,511	$16,620
2. Needs Analysis	11	0	0	0	0	0	0	0
3. Specifications	7	672	222	0	0	0	89	983
4. Select Server	8	768	253	0	0	0	102	1,124
5. Select Software	14	1,344	444	0	0	0	179	1,966
6. Select Cables	5	480	158	0	0	0	64	702
7. Purchasing	4	0	0	0	5,000	0	500	5,500
8. Manuals	8	768	253	0	0	0	102	1,124
9. Wire Offices	14	1,120	370	0	0	500	199	2,189
10. Set Up Server	5	480	158	0	0	0	64	702
11. Develop Training	16	1,536	507	750	0	0	279	3,072
12. Install Software	5	240	79	0	0	0	32	351
13. Connect Network	5	400	132	0	0	0	53	585
14. Train Users	10	960	317	2,000	0	250	353	3,879
15. Test/Debug	15	720	238	0	0	0	96	1,053
16. Acceptance	6	0	0	0	0	0	0	0
TOTALS	204	$20,848	$6,880	$2,750	$5,000	$750	$3,623	$39,851

Staff				Materials		Extra Charges
Project Manager	$20	per hour		Computer	$3,500	Overhead 33%
Assigned to Task 1	$160	per day		Software	750	
				Cables	250	
Computer Analyst	$12	per hour	(2 on team)	Connectors	500	G&A 10%
Assigned to remaining	$96	per day		TOTAL	$5,000	
Maintenance Staff	$10	per hour		**Contracts:**		
Assigned to Tasks 9, 13	$80	per day		Training		
				Development	$ 750	
				Train Users	2,000	

Fig. 9.2. *Revised Budget Worksheet for the sample LAN installation project.*

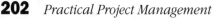

You might want to develop one final tool to help you manage and track project costs: a Budget Control Chart. The Budget Control Chart is a graph that shows cumulative project costs over the life of the project. At the beginning, you know planned costs, but not actual. As your project progresses, you can enter actual costs as they are incurred. Use that information to track your performance and anticipate potential problems (see fig. 9.3).

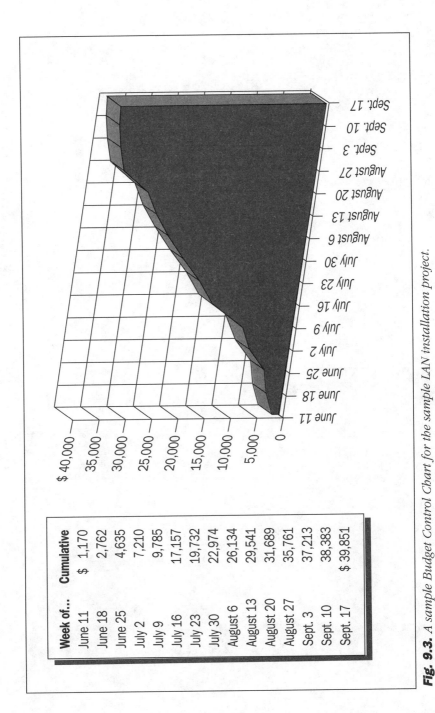

Week of...	Cumulative
June 11	$ 1,170
June 18	2,762
June 25	4,635
July 2	7,210
July 9	9,785
July 16	17,157
July 23	19,732
July 30	22,974
August 6	26,134
August 13	29,541
August 20	31,689
August 27	35,761
Sept. 3	37,213
Sept. 10	38,383
Sept. 17	$ 39,851

Fig. 9.3. *A sample Budget Control Chart for the sample LAN installation project.*

Managing
the Project

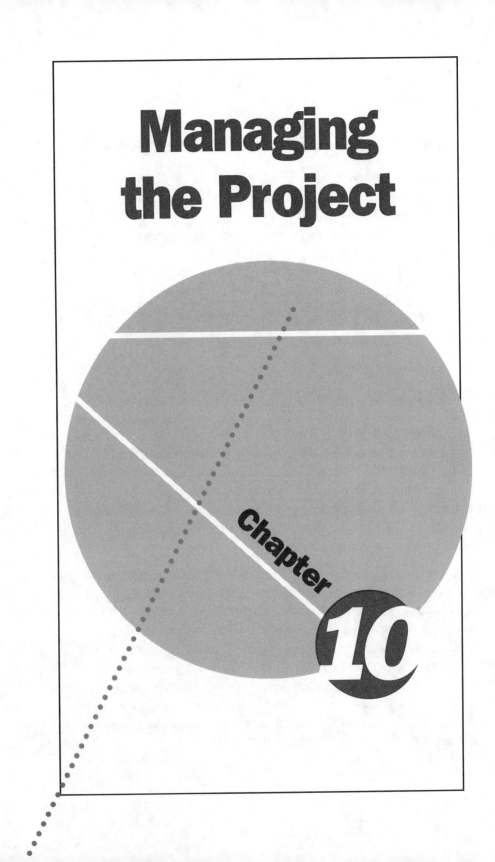

Chapter

10

Real-World Issues in Project Management

The strong concentration on planning in this book is no accident. The "Five Ps"—Prior Planning Prevents Poor Performance—is the most important single strategy you can follow to achieve your desired project outcome. It's perhaps overstating the case to say that prior planning prevents poor performance, since nothing can prevent all mishaps, but prior planning is the best tool you have to minimize problems when Godzilla is still a baby monster.

Projects are difficult to manage for two reasons:

- Projects take place within organizations.
- Projects have customers.

Both organizations and customers consist of people. People have different interests, goals, and styles. People don't, as a rule, check their humanity at the door when they punch in on the time clock. The project outcome they desire always has an emotional and personal content as well as a measurable and objective content. While the political aspects of projects may be a source of frustration (and occasional despair), you must develop strategies and tactics to deal with these real-world project management issues. In other words, get used to it.

Project management is, in a way, the ultimate management skill, because in addition to its own unique disciplines, project management includes all the other parts of conventional management: supervision, leadership, office politics, reports, meetings, and so on. Accordingly, no one never finishes the quest to become the perfect project manager. Therefore, make a commitment to lifelong learning, set a goal of continuous personal and professional improvement, and focus your learning on the things you need for tomorrow's success, not the things you needed for yesterday's accomplishments.

This is particularly good advice if you, like many project managers, came into the management ranks from a technical occupation. Most people in technical occupations are taught a respect for facts and logic, and therefore have a tendency to reject things that don't fit within a factual and logical context. Unfortunately, the same values and approaches do not work with human beings inside the dynamics of a typical organization. If you have problems in this area, then make that area of learning your next goal.

As you put the finishing touches on your project plan, verify each element of the schedule. Next, take a moment to appreciate the hard work and insight that has brought you to this point. Then take a deep breath. Now you're ready to actually manage the project.

What You Need to be a Great Project Manager

Like all managers, project managers must be leaders. They must know the business of their organizations. They must know about current concepts in management, from effective team approaches to empowerment, from TQM to MBO, from appraising performance to running meetings to preparing reports to working with other departments. They must be able to negotiate, to build consensus, to work and play well with others. Project management, like all management, requires good people skills.

Project management has unique elements as well. The technical aspects of project planning, the power of the Triple Constraints, the use of mathematical and statistical tools specific to the project world—all are part of the special world of project management.

In this chapter, you'll learn some of the management issues and problems of the project manager. To explore every single aspect of being an outstanding project manager would require including book-length chapters on teams, office politics, self-esteem, motivation, communications, and more. Obviously, that's not practical, so the pages that follow will focus on project management in general and touch briefly on the following issues: getting and using power and authority, team organization and management, motivation of team members, gaining support from other departments, and dealing with the problem of escalating project objectives. Understand that you must build and expand your library and tool set across a wide range of management disciplines.

Why Some Projects Fail...

Five Reasons for Failure

1. Lack of Project Manager authority

   "I must be a mushroom. They keep me in the dark, feed me manure, and then they can me."

2. Lack of team participation

   "If workers were smart, they'd be managers. Why ask them anything? After all, I'm the boss."

3. Bad reporting

   "Reports are just useless paperwork and an irrelevant management requirement. I fill out the form and then forget the form."

4. Lack of people skills

   "I don't thank people just for doing a good job. Doing a good job is what they get paid for."

5. Unrealistic goals and schedules

   "Your mission, should you decide to accept it ... if caught or killed, the Secretary will disavow any knowledge... "

...and Others Succeed

Three Reasons for Success

1. Committed teamwork

   "If anything goes bad, I did it. If anything goes semi-good, then we did it. If anything goes real good, then you did it. That's all it takes to get people to win football games."—*Paul "Bear" Bryant*

2. SMART Goals With Real Consensus

   "Specific, Measurable, Agreed-Upon, Realistic, and Time-Specific."

3. Use of project management tools as a means, not an end.

   "We have 562 pages of charts and graphs and still don't have a clue!"

How to Get and Use Power and Authority

You need power and authority to manage a project, but the traditional project manager usually receives less actual authority than he or she needs. This is often just a quirk of the organizational dynamic, but there's a serious additional agenda item here: real power and authority is not what others give you, but what you make and what you take.

Some people have an ethical concern about power. Is it morally acceptable to seek after power? To answer this question, let's use the engineering definition of power: energy that accomplishes work.

For example, you need gasoline to power your car. By itself, this is neither ethical nor unethical. How you get the gasoline is an ethical choice: you can buy it or you can steal it. The car will run when you put gasoline in it. By itself, that is neither ethical nor unethical. How you drive the car is an ethical choice: you can drive safely or disregard the rules of the road. What you do with the car is an ethical choice: you can use it as an ambulance or in a drive-by shooting. Gasoline and the running car by themselves are ethically neutral. The point? How you acquire and how you use power, and the purposes for which you use your power are subject to ethical rules. The mere fact of power considered alone is morally and ethically neutral.

In the world of people and organizations, the same logic applies. You need power to get any work done. Because you have a commitment to principled behavior, you need to know ways to acquire and use power that are ethical and appropriate.

If you take this as an endorsement of office politics, you are correct. How can this book endorse office politics, when they are so often at the core of project manager frustration and failure? Because they're real.

Office politics are a reality in any organization of three or more people. Office politics are simply what we use to describe the informal and sometimes emotionally-driven process of working out goals among people with conflicting interests. People want what they want, and you must deal with that.

Some people prefer the term "organizational dynamics" to describe this process, and that's a legitimate term. However, the more vibrant phrase "office politics" gives more of the flavor of the human conflict and personalities at its core. Organizational dynamics is more formal; office politics are informal—and the informal power structure in the organization is usually where the action takes place.

To understand how and where you currently fit, and how you might change your position if necessary, take the following quiz.

Quiz

The purpose and value of this quiz is to get you thinking about your current and official level of authority concerning your own project. Take the time to write your answers to each question fully, using extra paper. It's important to write your responses down; you'll see your ideas more clearly and be able to use them more effectively.

1. How would your boss define your current official role in managing your project? Is your official authority in writing, or informal?

   _____

   _____

   _____

   _____

2. List the resources (people, tools, systems) you need to accomplish the project goal. Then describe, specifically, how much official control you have over each resource.

   _____

   _____

   _____

3. What authority (if any) do you have to make or approve purchases, to negotiate and approve contracts, or to make other decisions that bind your organization legally or financially?

   _____

   _____

   _____

4. Do you select your own team members, are they selected for you, or is there a hybrid responsibility?

_____

_____

_____

_____

_____

_____

5. Does each key member of your project team report to you in a formal sense? If not, what level of authority do you possess (able to fire, reprimand, dismiss from team, etc.)? Do any members of your project team outrank you in the normal office hierarchy?

_____

_____

_____

_____

_____

6. Who's responsible for creating the plan, approving changes to the plan, maintaining the plan, and making work assignments based on the plan? If not you, where do you fit in?

_____

_____

_____

_____

_____

7. Do you have direct access to the ultimate customer or client for the project, or do you have to go through intervening management (internal or external)? Are you accepted by the customer as a technical authority? Do you regularly attend top-level meetings that impact the project?

_____

_____

_____

8. At what point do you have to gain the approval of others higher in the organization to make project-related decisions? Do you have enough respect and acceptance from higher authority for your recommendations to be seriously considered?

_____

_____

_____

9. List the key organizational players with concern for this project. Are there people in power positions who have agendas (hidden or clear) that affect the project outcome, resources, priority, or methodology?

_____

_____

_____

10. What is the relative priority of this project when compared to other projects within the organization? How do other organizational priorities affect your project?

_____

_____

_____

Now that you've completed the quiz, study your answers. If you're like many project managers, you may be somewhat depressed when you realize how little real authority you have. Here's where politics and power come into the equation: *the real power to manage your project is not what others give you, it's what you make and what you take.* You need this power to get the job done, and it's up to you to take the necessary steps. Here are some ways to achieve that power:

1. **Assertiveness is power.** Project managers must be assertive—not aggressive, not submissive. Good self-esteem is a project management skill. If you're given what seems to be an impossible project assignment, you have to say something about it. If the information you have isn't sufficient, you have to ask for additional information. If you aren't assertive and you lack self-esteem, others will walk on you. As Hawkeye Pierce once said to Frank Burns in an episode of *M*A*S*H*: "You invite abuse. It would be impolite not to accept it."

2. **Accomplishment is power.** "Nothing succeeds like success," the old saying goes, and this is true of project managers. Each time you achieve your goal, each time you get the job done when others could not, you gain power and influence proportional to the respect your accomplishment earned. The best of all political skills is to earn a reputation for outstanding work.

There are two caveats about accomplishment and respect:

- In war, there are many heroes, but only some get medals. Those are the ones with witnesses. If your great accomplishment goes unnoticed, it adds nothing to your power or influence.

- Nobody respects a braggart. If you're caught trumpeting your own horn too much, your accomplishments will be discounted. Successful managers master the high-wire act of calling appropriate attention to their success without slipping over the line into bragging.

3. **Knowledge is power.** When you earn a reputation for knowing what you're talking about, you gain power and influence. Separate but not unrelated to the idea of accomplishment, knowledge requires a commitment to study. Success expert Brian Tracy pointed out that if you read one book a week in your field, within three years you'd automatically be in the top 5 percent in knowledge. Why? Because during that time, you'd read roughly 150 books, far more than the average American who reads only one nonfiction book per year.

4. **Relationships are power.** Some people say "It's not what you know, it's who you know." Well, it's both. If you have knowledge, but lack people skills and good solid relationships, you'll find that you can put your knowledge to limited use. Of course, some people manage to get by for a while on people skills alone, without having anything of substance to offer, but this tends to come out in the long run. People with knowledge *and* good interpersonal skills succeed. These people are called leaders.

"If you want to know if you're a leader," Marilyn Moates Kennedy says in *Office Politics*, "just look back to see if anyone is following."

Leadership is different from supervision. Your boss can appoint you as a supervisor, but only your staff can accept you as a leader. People voluntarily choose to follow leaders, individuals who are charismatic, who are skilled negotiators, and who display self-confidence.

One of the tapes in the American Management Association tape series *Success Essentials* includes a discussion of how to manage problem employees. That tape yields a key insight into why some employees don't do what they're supposed to do. The reason is simple—they believe that doing things your way won't meet their needs. Marilyn Moates Kennedy defined office politics by the same standard: "What is it exactly that I can do for you that will make you want to do it my way?"

5. **Initiative is power.** One quick way to determine the limits of your authority is simply to do it anyway and see what happens, on the grounds that it's often easier to get forgiveness than permission.

This is *not* an endorsement to blindly disregard rules and do whatever you want—quite the contrary. One of the rules of management of any sort is that management involves risk. If the problem has one right answer, if the problem is such that all the facts are available, if the problem fits neatly within your official purview, then it's a simple problem. But managers aren't paid to handle the simple problems. (Enjoy them when you have them though.)

Managers are paid to handle the tougher problems. A tough problem may have many answers—sometimes none of them absolutely right. And with a tough problem, many key facts may be unavailable and sometimes impossible to obtain. A tough problem has unclear lines of authority. Intelligent risk-taking, creativity, and good judgment are the fundamental management skills.

One project manager's boss once told him, "If I haven't had to call you down for exceeding your authority, you're demonstrating that you don't have a need for any more."

When the ball lands in your lap, it's your ball. Whether you keep it or pass it, it's yours right now.

6. **People skills are power.** The ability to work and play well with others, which we remember so well from our childhood report cards, is still an important element in our adulthood, especially as project managers.

There are at least two "universal" professions—sales and negotiation. These are professions to which we all belong regardless of our official fields. We're all in the sales business because we must persuade others to do our bidding. We're all in the negotiation business because, as top negotiation author Roger Dawson said, "Everything you want right now is owned or controlled by someone else."

To get what you want, remember that everybody's tuned in to the world's most popular radio station, WII-FM . . . the "**W**hat's **I**n **I**t **F**or **M**e" radio network. Armed with this realization, you must approach sales and negotiation from the point of view of Mick Jagger, "You can't always get what you want, but if you try real hard, you might just get what you need." That's the win/win approach.

The biggest insight for effective sales and negotiation is that you have two ears but only one mouth—and that's a good ratio. Most people mistakenly associate effective sales and negotiation with being a fast and aggressive talker, but the reality is that great persuaders are great listeners. If I am to give you what you need in order to get what I need, I first have to understand what it is that you need.

7. **Communication is power.** "If you don't ask, you don't get." Communication is part of all these power issues. The art of communication involves the ability to articulate your goals and desires, to put them across in persuasive and positive language, to get your message understood. You must be understood before you can gain acceptance and agreement.

8. **Understanding is power.** Who are the key players in this project, what are their relative powers, and what do they want? You can puzzle out many of the things that motivate people by using the following techniques:

- Put yourself in their shoes and look at the problem from their perspective. What will success for the project mean for them? Does it advance their career or harm it? What personal benefits do they acquire from the project's success or failure?

- People are motivated to achieve their own self-interests. If a team member complains and whines every time you give him or her a work assignment, you may get so annoyed that you give the assignments to a more positive team member. The whiner then achieves his or her immediate goal.

- More people think short-term than long-term. When the whiner is subsequently passed over for a promotion, he or she is often shocked. The short-term goal has been achieved at the cost of the long-term goal.

In an experiment to improve child safety, young children were put in a room with various bottles filled with harmless liquids. Some were marked with the skull and crossbones "poison" symbol. Others were marked with a variety of other signs. The skull and crossbones did not dissuade children from drinking from the bottle. It was exotic and forbidden, and therefore tempting. The green "Mr. Yuck" face did discourage the children. Notice that the threat of long-term death was much less persuasive than the idea of an immediate unpleasant taste. Quite a few adults still operate at this level of thinking.

Team Organization and Management Issues

Teams are at the center of much current management thinking. Teams are the new work unit as—in Alvin Toffler's phrase—business moves from the "bureaucracy" of the past to the "adhocracy" of the future. Teams are dynamically different from the conventional boss/worker relationships of the past, and they require a different management approach. Concepts like "empowerment" (which is too often confused with "abandonment") are particularly significant to project managers. This is because project mangers require the active participation of team members to achieve significant goals.

While the reality of project management is often that your team is a given, it's clearly ideal to select team members strategically. Even if you have limited power to select your team members, work through these issues. You may need to acquire certain skills outside the core team. You may also identify some likely management issues affecting team performance. You may not be able to solve all your problems in advance, but advance warning is helpful.

The two factors in selecting team members are skills and personality.

The initial draft of the project tasks should help you determine the skills you'll require of team members. Make a master skill list. As you choose team members, check off their skills against your skill list. In the ideal team, you should have at least two people (one a backup) with each critical skill, so that in the event you lose a key member during the project's life span, you'll have options. Cross-training is useful; so is preassigning backups so that each team member keeps his or her backup abreast of critical details.

Once you've ascertained that a prospective team member has the fundamental skills required to do the work, favor personality over additional skill. In many cases, the ability to work with others toward a common goal is more important than marginally better skills. Is the person articulate? Assertive rather than aggressive or submissive? Can the person attend a meeting and contribute to it—neither dominating it nor sitting there like a bump on a log? Does the person have a strong work ethic? Does the person understand and support the project's goals?

Always interview team members—even if you don't control their hiring. Here are two areas you should ask about:

- **Their background.** Even if you've worked with these people for years, you may be surprised to find out about skills they possess that they've never had to use in the current work environment. Does your boss know everything that you've ever done?

- **Their goals within the organization and within the project.** Knowing their goals is key to knowing what motivates them. To give people what they want, you must know what they want.

Next, think about team organization. This is influenced by the situation. Does your team need a formal structure where each member has clearly defined authority and responsibilities. A construction project is a good example of a project requiring a formal team structure. Does it need an informal, *ad hoc* structure that adapts to changing circumstances? R&D efforts lend themselves to this loose type of structure. Are team members in the same physical location, or are they spread out geographically? Will they have a long-term working relationship, or are they together only for this brief project?

Motivating People to Achieve

Have you ever met an unmotivated person?

When trainers ask that question at management seminars, they get an enthusiastic sea of hands saying "Yes!" A lack of apparent motivation in co-workers and team members is a constant irritant to other team members and managers.

But rephrase the question and ask: Have you ever had a co-worker who spent more time and energy each day scheming to get out of work than it would take simply to finish the work and get it over with? Of course! Such people abound in the workplace. So, back to the original question: Are they unmotivated? Hardly. The issue in motivation is not whether people have it (they do), but *what* motivates them.

The principles of effective motivation can be summarized in the GREAT model:

Goals

Roles

Expectations

Attitudes

Time

Goals. Have you ever been in a situation where no one in the group could decide where to go for dinner? "I dunno. Where do you wanna go?" This back-and-forth volley lasts until someone says assertively, "Let's go to _____."

One way to motivate desired behavior is to be assertive and clear about what you want and where you're going. A person with strong, clear goals gets more cooperation and support than someone without goals.

Roles. People find it easier to cooperate when they know where they stand and what their responsibilities are. There's comfort in clarity. People unsure of their roles and their situation often yield to fear, and fear destroys positive motivation.

Expectations. People need to know what you expect of them, and you need to set those expectations high to get maximum results. Make your expectations clear from the outset, and give feedback on how to meet them. Remember as you're offering input that positive feedback is even more helpful than negative feedback. Catch team members doing things right and tell them about it—early and often.

Attitudes. The most important attitude on your team is your own. Like it or not, choose it or not, you *are* a role model. No one works harder than you, cares more than you, has more discipline than you, is more positive than you. Your attitude becomes the upper speed limit for your team. Make sure you manage your own morale and keep it high. (Sometimes you have to be a good actor, even to the point of faking a better attitude than you feel inside. A bad attitude and a sense of futility on your part can rob your project of any hope.)

Time. Whether time is the driver or not, time is always of the essence. If there's absolutely no time pressure, then the project will be completed when team members get around to it, which may be never. Promote a sense of urgency to give your team energy.

Getting Support From Other Departments

Every course on Total Quality Management (TQM) contains a segment on the "internal customer"—someone to whom you give work or from whom you get work. In general terms, your customers want something from you (a work output) and you want something in return (with an external customer, it's often money). Internal customers want work output from you, and you want work output from them.

In the external world, customers keep you in business by creating the demand for the products and services you supply. This is true obviously in the for-profit sector, but it's also true in the not-for-profit sector. In the internal world, other departments make your projects possible because unless the project is small, you normally must gain the willing cooperation of other departments that you neither supervise nor control in order to get the work done.

Frankly, this concept can be expressed in political terms. You want something from another department and they want something from you. For example, if you need the Purchasing department to accelerate your requisitions so you can meet the schedule, you need their cooperation. But they're not thrilled with the extra work demands. How do you get their cooperation?

The best approach is to start far in advance of need. Build good relationships early. In the case of the Purchasing department, you might go for a visit. "What could we do better to make your life easier?" you ask.

They might reply that you're not filling out the requisition forms correctly, not giving them enough lead time, or trying to specify vendors instead of letting them follow their policies. All too often, you may discover that you're making other people's lives miserable and difficult without meaning to, simply because you don't know any better. Learning to fill out the forms right might take some extra short-term effort, but it will likely speed up forms completion and will definitely speed up Purchasing's response time.

Managing other departments is the same as managing team members who don't formally report to you. Always ask Marilyn Moates Kennedy's question: What can I do for you that will make you want to do it my way?

Coping With the Escalating Objective

Although certain management problems can affect any project manager in any situation at any time, one particular nightmare that stands out is the escalating project objective. This occurs when the initial project objective, although properly approved and signed off by the customer, starts creeping upward as the project progresses. Time compresses, the budget shrinks, and performance criteria increase.

Whether change orders are formal or informal, they tend to be a common part of the project management experience. It's no use saying it shouldn't be that way (although it shouldn't): you must instead learn how to cope with it.

Try some or all of the following techniques to cope with project objectives that expand after the project is underway.

1. **Do the entire Triple Constraints process.** If you haven't fully negotiated and explored the Triple Constraints using the process described in Chapter 2, this may be the source of some of your problems. Too many project managers rush ahead before identifying the underlying project reason and the management, organizational, and customer issues that influence it.

2. **Find out who has an interest in the outcome.** Remember from the Triple Constraints process that a project has a central objective but often has secondary objectives that are the related interests of all those who form the project constituency. You must discover who your project constituency is, interview them, find out their goals and perceptions, and integrate as many of their goals as possible without compromising the central objective.

   Don't forget the personal as well as the external motivations.

3. **Put it in writing and shop it around.** A good goal is a written goal. Make sure to inform people in advance and in writing of the goal and give them an early opportunity to challenge that goal. Although negotiating a workable compromise can be difficult, it's much easier than coping with a major change order late in the project that virtually guarantees disaster.

   Although people can still change a written goal, it's harder than changing an unwritten goal.

4. **Show others your plans, schedules, and budgets.** You can't take for granted that others in management will have the same level of understanding of the consequences of a proposed project change that you have. Document the consequences of a change clearly and objectively (no whining!).

   When a change is requested, print out a current plan and budget. Next, integrate the change into the existing schedule and print out the revised plan and budget. Third, brainstorm positive and proactive ways of achieving the new goal in the best possible way. Revise the schedule and budget to accommodate the change. Print that out.

Now, go to management and/or the customer. Show them the three versions:

1. No change

2. Integrating the change and going in a straight line

3. Your best ideas about how to integrate the change and still achieve the rest of the time/budget/performance goals.

Ask whether they have better suggestions.

Perhaps they do have better suggestions—be positive and agreeable when you adopt them. Perhaps seeing the consequences clearly will make them realize that the change isn't wise or possible. It's easier for people to save face and back down if you're being positive. Without intending it, you can all too easily give the impression that you think they're all stupid and incompetent with no clue as to the consequences of the change. Always give people the opportunity to save face.

Another point to remember is that management has a tendency to believe, based on much real-world experience, that employees usually aren't proactive about change, but instead look for ways to prove that change is impossible. Don't play into that preconceived notion. Always be as positive as you can about change.

5. **Build change into the process.** In many projects, change orders are inevitable because of the nature of the work. It may not be possible to identify all the real needs until the work has progressed to a certain point. In this case, you need to build change into the process.

   Set milestones in your project schedule for "customer review and expectation development" and tasks for "integration of requirements changes" and "redevelopment to accommodate changes." Build this into your initial schedule and budget. If it's inevitable, it's inevitable. Plan for it.

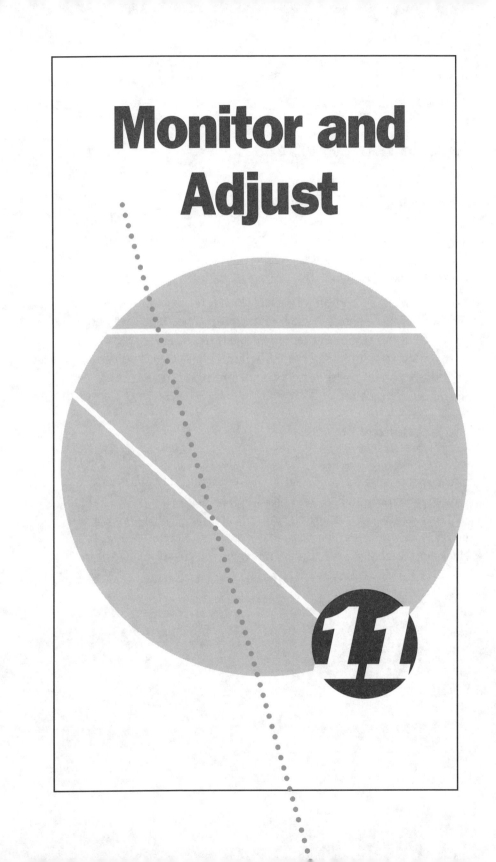

Monitor and
Adjust

11

How to Track Progress

If you sit in your office waiting for people to bring you the information you need to stay updated about your project, you'll have a long and lonely wait ahead of you. To keep Godzilla out of Tokyo, you must be proactive in monitoring project events. When you're proactive, you can act early, when options are strongest, to solve inevitable project problems.

You can begin your monitoring process during your planning by developing the Control Point Identification Chart (see fig 5.9 on page 96), a brainstorming record of what might go wrong (and right), how you could catch it early, and what you could do about it. You can build in milestones and reporting periods throughout your project.

Project Control Chart

To build a Project Control Chart, take the task list from the plan and create a table, as in Table 11.1. Add actual time and budget data as they accumulate, and monitor the variance. *(Note:* Budget variance is always significant; time variance is only significant on critical tasks or when variance exceeds available slack. Both free slack and total slack are listed on the Project Control Chart.)

Table 11.1 Project Control Chart

Task	F. Slack	T. Slack	Schedule	Actual	Var.	Budget	Actual	Var.
1. Project Mgmt.			71		0	$16,620		$0
2. Needs Analysis			11		0	0		0
3. Specifications			7		0	983		0
4. Select Server	0.63	1	8		0	1,124		0
5. Select Software			14		0	1,966		0
6. Select Cables	1	1	5		0	702		0
7. Purchasing			4		0	5,500		0
8. Manuals	2.63	6	8		0	1,124		0
9. Wire Offices			14		0	2,189		0
10. Set Up Server	0.63	4	5		0	702		0
11. Develop Training	0.63	4	16		0	3,072		0
12. Install Software	4	4	5		0	351		0
13. Connect Network			5		0	585		0
14. Train Users	4	4	10		0	3,879		0
15. Test/Debug			15		0	1,053		0
16. Acceptance			6		0	0		0
TOTALS	N/A	N/A	204	N/A	0	$39,851	N/A	$0

Milestone Chart

You can also build a Milestone Chart. This is a checklist of key events and their scheduled completion dates. Key events are either points requiring approval to proceed or measurable and verifiable accomplishments that tell you the work is going well.

Table 11.2 Milestone Chart

Milestone	Scheduled	Actual
Purchasing Decisions Made	June 19	
Equipment Delivery	June 25	
Wires in Wall	August 11	
Network Connected	August 18	
Users Trained	September 4	
Fully Tested	September 8	
Accepted	September 19	

Reporting System

You can set up a reporting system. Reporting systems, by their nature, must be customized around the project and organization. The most important point about a good reporting system is that people follow it. Use these principles:

1. **Don't ask for information you don't need.** Think about how you will use each bit of information in your report.

2. **Design your own report formats.** Combat the natural human tendency to tell you what you want to hear, or to make the reporter look good.

3. **Use graphics when possible.** A picture is worth a thousand words, particularly where reports are concerned. People take money, time, and other quantifiable variables far more seriously if they are visually striking.

Meeting Schedule

You can set up a meeting schedule, but remember that although meetings may be necessary, they're not automatically effective. Many project managers assume that everyone knows how to have a meeting, and then they're frequently surprised. As a manager, take meetings seriously—and expect others to do so as well. Use these principles to plan your meeting schedule.

1. **Make sure enough has changed to justify a new meeting.** You can schedule meetings along with milestones or on a regular basis, but choose the frequency based on progress. If all your tasks are weekly, daily meetings are suspect.

2. **Have an agenda and purpose for each meeting.** Although most managers know that agendas are important, many don't use them. When people who will be attending the meeting know what the meeting is for and know how to prepare, they are more likely to be productive.

3. **Send out an action summary after each meeting.** Skip minutes, which are mostly useless. An action summary lists decisions and work assignments made during the meeting.

4. **Model desired behavior.** Arrive on time, take the business of the meeting seriously, and work toward an on-time and on-target conclusion.

Monitoring System

You can set up a monitoring system, including inspections, progress reviews, tests, audits, and other techniques. Use your plan as a guide, and insist that all reviews involve reference to the plan.

The key issue in monitoring is that you realize its importance to project success. Keep your eye on the ball from project start to project finish.

Earned Value Method

Certain large projects, especially those in construction and engineering, use the Earned Value Method. The Earned Value Method is used in part to determine interim payments when work is being performed on contract for a client. The Earned Value Method is a way of showing schedule variance in monetary terms—if you're late, it affects your payment. You should probably use the Earned Value Method only if you're required to do so by a customer, then study it in more detail. This brief explanation is only to help you recognize the terminology and concepts should you encounter them in your projects.

Here are some of the terms you'll need to understand to work with the Earned Value Method:

The *Budgeted Cost of Work Scheduled (BCWS)* is the original budget estimate for a given task.

The *Actual Cost of Work Performed (ACWP)* is the actual cost of performing the given task.

The *Budgeted Cost of Work Performed (BCWP)* is the "earned value"—a measure of the dollar value of the work actually performed to date.

The *Schedule Variance* is expressed as BCWP minus BCWS, which shows schedule variance in monetary terms.

For example, if Task 7 had a BCWS of $6,000 and was only 50 percent complete at the deadline, it would have a BCWP of $6,000 x 50 percent, or $3,000. If the ACWP to that point were $4,000, you'd be $1,000 over current budget, but you'd be looking at a $2,000 budget overage when you finished (if $4,000 is 50 percent complete, then the expected ACWP is $8,000). The schedule variance expressed in monetary terms is -$3,000, which is how much the customer will deduct from the current payment due.

Tracking Gantt—A Powerful Tool

Most of the techniques described so far in this chapter can be used for a variety of work situations, not just for projects. The Gantt Chart proves useful yet again as a visual way of measuring progress against schedule and forecasting the impact of problems on project goals.

To make a Tracking Gantt Chart, take the original plan and draw an extra line for each task. That line will represent the actual time each task took. Using the dependency sequence, you can quickly analyze the consequences of any task slippage. If you're a software user, your program may have the ability to create a Tracking Gantt automatically.

Return now to the simpler of your sample projects to explore this technique. In the Chapter 8 exercise, you determined the Critical Path for your project to buy a word processing system. The Critical Path consisted of tasks 1-2-4-5-7-8 for a total of 19 working days.

In figure 11.1, you see the project laid out as a Tracking Gantt. You'll see two bars for each task: the upper bar in each pair is either the actual time it took to perform the task, or a forecast of the time span for tasks that haven't yet occurred.

Three tasks have a completion factor of 100 percent: tasks 1, 2, and 3. That means they are complete. The remaining tasks have a completion factor of 0 percent, which means they have not yet been started. Tasks 1 and 3 took the scheduled amount of time. Task 2, unfortunately, did not. It was scheduled to take 5 working days, but has actually taken 8 working days. (Be sure to deduct weekends from your schedule—unless your project operates 7 days a week.)

Because Task 2 was a critical task, the consequences are severe: Task 4, scheduled to begin July 3, now begins July 6 because it is still dependent on the finish of Task 2. Tasks 5 and 6 are pushed out, and so are Tasks 7 and 8. Unless you take some kind of action, your 19-day project will take a total of 22 days—three days over, which (not coincidentally) is the Task 2 lateness.

Time and money are usually flip sides of the same coin in projects (unless you supervise volunteers). Now consider the impact of the project delay on your budget situation. Assume that each staff member earns $100 per day, one person does each job full time, and the hardware/software combination cost is $3,000. Lag time costs $75 per day (maintenance and overhead costs). (Omit staff overhead and G&A from this example.) This gives you the Budget Control Chart shown in figure 11.2.

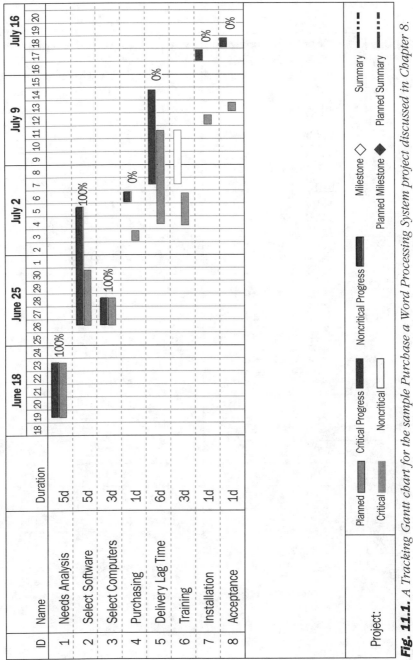

Fig. 11.1. A Tracking Gantt chart for the sample Purchase a Word Processing System project discussed in Chapter 8.

Plan			Actual		
Day	Cost	Cumulative	Day	Cost	Cumulative
1	$100	$100	1	$100	$100
2	$100	$200	2	$100	$200
3	$100	$300	3	$100	$300
4	$100	$400	4	$100	$400
5	$100	$500	5	$100	$500
6	$200	$700	6	$200	$700
7	$200	$900	7	$200	$900
8	$200	$1,100	8	$200	$1,100
9	$100	$1,200	9	$100	$1,200
10	$100	$1,300	10	$100	$1,300
11	$3,100	$4,400	11	$100	$1,400
12	$175	$4,575	12	$100	$1,500
13	$175	$4,750	13	$100	$1,600
14	$175	$4,925	14	$3,100	$4,700
15	$75	$5,000	15	$175	$4,875
16	$75	$5,075	16	$175	$5,050
17	$75	$5,150	17	$175	$5,225
18	$100	$5,250	18	$75	$5,300
19	$100	$5,350	19	$75	$5,375
20	End	$5,350	20	$75	$5,450
21			21	$100	$5,550
22			22	$100	$5,650

Fig. 11.2. *The Budget Control Chart for the Word Processing System project.*

You'll notice that on Day 13, you're in very good shape financially—$3,000 under budget (see fig. 11.3). Of course, that's cash flow, not budget, since the purchasing has only been postponed, not eliminated. Assuming that nothing else goes wrong, you currently expect to end the project three days late and $300 over budget ($100 a day for each staff member's salary).

What can you do? Quite a lot, actually. You can't change the past, but you can modify every aspect of the rest of the project in the same way you planned it in the first place. All the techniques you learned earlier for shortening time and lowering budget are applicable. Now search the remaining project for opportunities to save time and/or money and to get back on schedule.

One way to save three days and $300 would be to eliminate Task 6, "Training" (redefine performance criteria). You could argue that buying and installing the computer doesn't require training the eventual user. Unfortunately, eliminating "Training" doesn't save you any days because "Training" isn't a critical path task.

However, as you look through the mail order catalog from which you plan to buy the computer, you discover that the company has an option for overnight delivery. In fact, it has two: two-day service for an extra $200, and one-day service for an extra $300. This is a "crash time" opportunity.

Since "Delivery Lag Time" is a Critical Path task, speeding it up should make a difference. Should you spend $200 to save three days or $300 to save five days? (These are two crash slope choices, which are written "-4, $200" and "-5, $300.")

You may find that exploring the consequences of using crash analysis is easier on a PERT chart. The three sections of fig. 11.4 show the three options:

The first PERT chart shows that if you do nothing, the time from Purchasing through Acceptance will take nine days. (The critical path is highlighted with thicker lines.)

The second PERT chart shows the impact of going with the -5, $300 overnight delivery option. The time from Purchasing through Delivery and Installation to Acceptance is 4 days, but the time from Purchasing through Training to Acceptance is 5 days. The Critical Path has changed! It takes five days to get through these tasks. (The total project time, however, is 18 days: you're going to end up a day ahead of schedule! See fig. 11.5)

The third PERT chart shows the impact of going with the -4, $200 second-day delivery option. The time from Purchasing through Delivery and Installation to Acceptance is 5 days—and so is the time to get there through Training! In other words, there are now *two* critical paths—and this project phase takes five days either way! You still end up with an 18-day total time estimate.

Common sense says that overnight delivery is a day faster than second-day delivery, but the PERT chart shows that in this case there is no time difference. (Some project managers might argue that paying the extra $100 is a good idea because Installation might be troublesome. That's a legitimate argument if you feel that the risk justifies the expense. However, you're not spending the $100 to save time; you're spending it for a different purpose: risk reduction.)

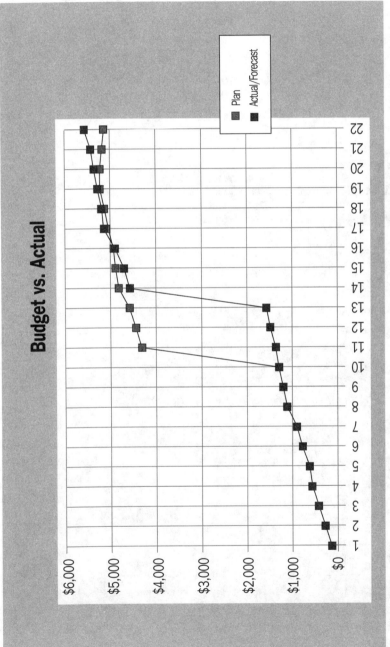

Fig. 11.3. *Graphical representation of the budget versus actual amounts spent for the Word Processing System project.*

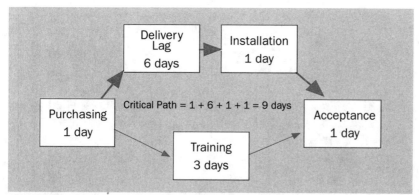

Fig. 11.4a. *The expected project schedule if nothing is done.*

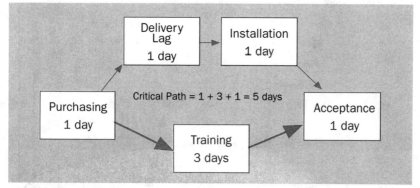

Fig. 11.4b. *Paying for overnight delivery. Notice the Critical Path has changed.*

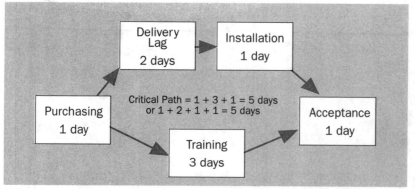

Fig. 11.4c. *Paying for second-day delivery. Notice there are now two Critical Paths.*

Now consider the budget. In your first option, you spent an extra $300, but the budget variance is now only $225 over budget. You got $75 of the overage back in saved labor costs while cutting your total project time by one day! (See figs. 11.6 and 11.7.)

You spent an extra $200 in your second option to get back on your planned schedule. Your total budget variance is now only $175 over—to achieve the same outcome! (See figs. 11.8 and 11.9.)

In some cases, you'll find that spending extra money you don't have can actually lower total budget and time. The reason for this, of course, is that time and money are flip sides of the same coin.

As you can see, the Tracking Gantt is not only a powerful tool for monitoring and control, it's also an important element in your problem-solving strategy.

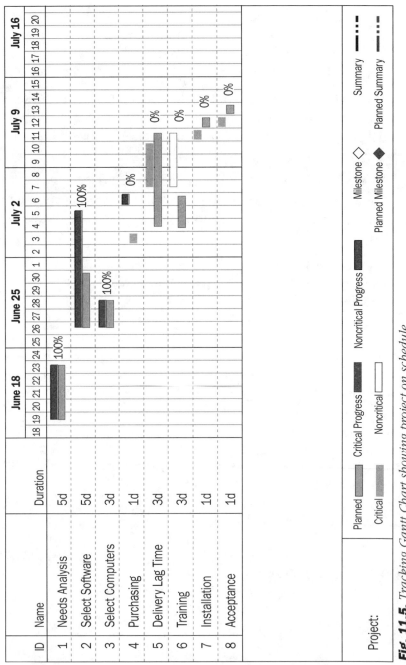

Fig. 11.5. *Tracking Gantt Chart showing project on schedule.*

Plan			Actual		
Day	Cost	Cumulative	Day	Cost	Cumulative
1	$100	$100	1	$100	$100
2	$100	$200	2	$100	$200
3	$100	$300	3	$100	$300
4	$100	$400	4	$100	$400
5	$100	$500	5	$100	$500
6	$200	$700	6	$200	$700
7	$200	$900	7	$200	$900
8	$200	$1,100	8	$200	$1,100
9	$100	$1,200	9	$100	$1,200
10	$100	$1,300	10	$100	$1,300
11	$3,100	$4,400	11	$100	$1,400
12	$175	$4,575	12	$100	$1,500
13	$175	$4,750	13	$100	$1,600
14	$175	$4,925	14	$3,100	$4,700
15	$75	$5,000	15	$475	$5,175
16	$75	$5,075	16	$200	$5,375
17	$75	$5,150	17	$100	$5,475
18	$100	$5,250	18	$100	$5,575
19	$100	$5,350	19	End	$5,575
20	End	$5,350	20		$5,575
21			21		
22			22		

Fig. 11.6. Budget Control Chart reflecting new budget variance using overnight delivery.

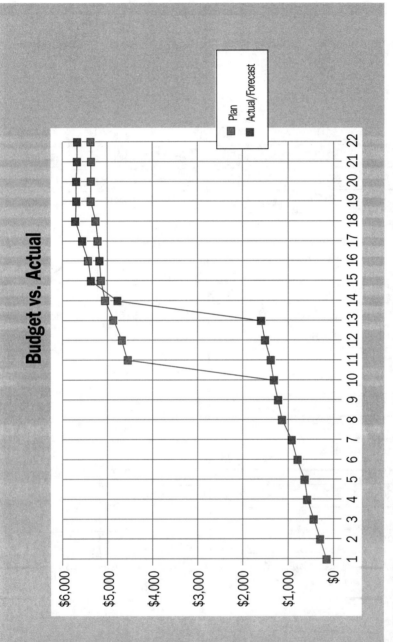

Fig. 11.7. *Speeding up system delivery using Option 1 reduces budget overage by $75.*

Plan			Actual		
Day	Cost	Cumulative	Day	Cost	Cumulative
1	$100	$100	1	$100	$100
2	$100	$200	2	$100	$200
3	$100	$300	3	$100	$300
4	$100	$400	4	$100	$400
5	$100	$500	5	$100	$500
6	$200	$700	6	$200	$700
7	$200	$900	7	$200	$900
8	$200	$1,100	8	$200	$1,100
9	$100	$1,200	9	$100	$1,200
10	$100	$1,300	10	$100	$1,300
11	$3,100	$4,400	11	$100	$1,400
12	$175	$4,575	12	$100	$1,500
13	$175	$4,750	13	$100	$1,600
14	$175	$4,925	14	$3,100	$4,700
15	$75	$5,000	15	$375	$5,075
16	$75	$5,075	16	$175	$5,250
17	$75	$5,150	17	$175	$5,425
18	$100	$5,250	18	$100	$5,525
19	$100	$5,350	19	End	$5,525
20	End	$5,350	20		
21			21		
22			22		

Fig. 11.8. *Budget Control Chart reflecting budget variance using Option 2.*

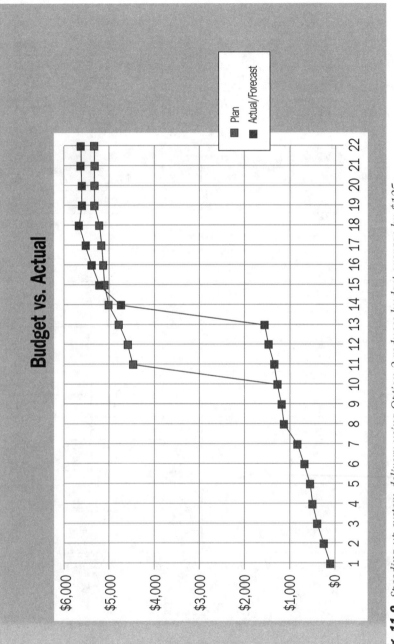

Budget vs. Actual

■ Plan
■ Actual/Forecast

Fig. 11.9. Speeding up system delivery using Option 2 reduces budget overage by $125.

Problem-Solving Strategies

The first and best way to eliminate project problems is to thoroughly and carefully plan. Realistically, you'll never be able to plan so perfectly to eliminate all problems. It's when problems arise that project managers earn their money. Here are some problem-solving strategies that work:

Define the real problem. The first element in an effective problem-solving strategy is to define the problem. The real problem isn't necessarily the core problem. Use the "Five Whys" technique to look behind the problem. Ask "why" the visible problem occurred. When you get a reason, ask why that happened, and so on. Five "whys" will get you closer to the core problem, the one that must ultimately be solved. (Five is a guideline, not an absolute number.)

Return to the Triple Constraints and the ultimate reason for doing the project in the first place. Your problem is a real problem if and only if it threatens that reason. If the Critical Path has slipped, and time is not the driver, you might not be too concerned about correcting it. If you are over budget, and budget is the weak constraint, being overbudget may be superior to the alternatives. If a performance standard hasn't been achieved, the question you have to ask is how that might affect real quality—that is, what the customer needs, wants, or expects.

Verify that the driver and weak constraint are still in the right order. Once you've properly determined constraint order, it doesn't tend to slip around (if it does, that suggests it may not have been properly defined in the first place). However, major changes in the external environment (new owners, change in customers, a stock market crash) can change constraint order, and with it the dynamics of your project. Check for flexibility in the weak constraint and, if possible, use that flexibility as a problem-solving tool.

Brainstorm options. When you need a great idea, start with a lot of ideas. The goal of brainstorming is to gather a large number of ideas that range from sensible to off-the-wall. Prefer quantity of ideas to quality of ideas in this process. Set a rule that no one is to evaluate or comment on ideas. Judging ideas at this stage cuts off free thinking.

Try some of these brainstorming techniques:

1. Print the subject in big letters on a blackboard or flip chart.

2. Set a goal for total ideas (say, 100), and run the session until that number of ideas is achieved. (Remember, they don't have to be good ones.)

3. Progress in a "round robin" style, calling on each participant in turn, so that big talkers don't dominate the process. Each team member may offer only one idea per turn. If a participant doesn't have an idea on a given round, that person passes.

4. Record all ideas, even jokes, silly ideas, or off-the-wall suggestions. Remember, no criticism is allowed.

5. Encourage synergy: Build on ideas already on the flip chart.

6. Be patient with the process. Encourage looseness, movement, and think time.

Narrow the field. After the brainstorming session, reduce the total number of ideas to a workable size and build team consensus toward a solution. Use the multivoting technique to do this. Here's how it works.

1. Number the brainstormed items.

2. Consider each item in order, allowing team members to clarify, add, combine, or delete items. (To combine or delete, you must have 100 percent group agreement. Otherwise, let the ideas stand for this round.)

3. Team members may lobby for their favorite ideas. Lobbying must be positive; that is, it must support an item. No criticism is allowed.

4. Use a show of hands to vote for keeping each item. Team members may vote for as many items as they want. Cut items that don't receive significant group support.

5. If there are still too many ideas to consider sensibly, give each team member half as many votes as there are ideas remaining, and repeat step four with the limited votes. Repeat this until the idea list is reduced to a manageable size.

Build consensus toward a solution. The Nominal Group Technique (NGT) is a powerful strategy for building consensus. Give each member a voting card and the following instructions:

1. Write the words "Item" and "Rank" on each card.

2. List your top five ideas by number under "Item."

3. Rank the ideas by your priority, "5" for the highest priority, "1" for the lowest.

4. Now, collect the cards and total up rankings and number of responses to determine priority. Example: If an idea got three #1 votes and two #2 votes, it receives 7 points, since $[(3x1)+(2x2)]=7$. Lower scores are better. Record the scores for the group and repeat to eliminate ties.

The reason for this technique is that while there may be disagreement on the best idea, there may be a strong consensus on the second best. NGT ensures that the idea with the widest group support is chosen.

Examine the solution carefully. Use Force Field Analysis to explore the solution in detail. Set up the format shown in figure 11.10 on a blackboard or flip chart. Then use brainstorming to identify "driving" and "restraining" forces. *Driving forces* support the solution; *restraining forces* work against the solution.

Use brainstorming and NGT to prioritize the forces you come up with, look for solutions to any new problems you identify, and continue until you have developed a workable solution.

Force Field Analysis	
Driving Forces	Restraining Forces

Fig. 11.10. Using Force Field Analysis, team members can evaluate the reasons for adopting a solution or identifying reasons a recommended solution may not work.

General Techniques for Saving Time and Money

The toolbox of the experienced project manager is packed with techniques that can be applied to a wide variety of situations. When you're stuck and looking for answers, test each of the following ideas as a potential source.

Renegotiate the project requirements. If you've reached a point in the project where you have done the best you can and there's no way to achieve the desired outcome, it's time to renegotiate with the project originators. This is hard to do. You may feel embarrassed and/or powerless. After all, you are the captain of this sinking ship—not the best position to negotiate from.

Don't underestimate your position. Strong negotiators know how to get the best terms even under these circumstances. Your position is powerful, indeed. The reality is that you've spent the time and money. It's gone. The customer's choice is to get nothing for the time and money invested, or to spend extra time and money (or alter ideal performance standards) to get something. Something is better than nothing in most cases.

This isn't shameful or manipulative—it's simply factual. Although you're committed to quality and excellence, don't let "perfect" become the enemy of good. If you can't achieve the customer's ideal goal, work with the customer to find the best goal you can achieve to meet as many of the customer's needs as possible. Don't let personal shame or any other emotions undercut you. In the long run, they don't do you or your customer any favors.

Recover later. The Tracking Gantt analysis showed a strategy for later recovery. In your initial planning process, you may discover crash time options or paralleling options that are marginal. Perhaps they cost too much, or increase risk unnecessarily. Keep them in your pocket for later and have some back-up solutions to help you solve your problems.

Narrow the project scope. As you learned on the Moon Project in Chapter 2, a project normally has one or two central, overriding objectives and a host of secondary objectives that are desirable, but not essential. If you discover that your schedule is being pushed up because of certain circumstances (e.g., in the case of the moon shot example, the Soviet program going into overdrive), it's time to narrow the project scope. Evaluate all the performance standards, determine which can't be compromised without fundamentally destroying the project, and cut the rest back.

Throw more resources at it. The crash technique may solve your problems. Look for opportunities where using additional resources would reduce time on the Critical Path (but not in excess of slack on parallel lines—that doesn't accomplish anything). Depending on penalties for noncompletion or other costs to the project, paying for extra resources to get the job done may even save money.

Accept substitutions. Go through your shopping list and identify whether you really need the turbocharged name-brand version, or whether the off-brand without the gold-plated sockets would meet the critical performance objectives.

Work with your subcontractors. Improve your negotiating position by making sure you have explored alternate sources for the goods and services you require. Don't make yourself a hostage unnecessarily. You can go beyond the contract to offer incentives for better time and quality. You can simply be assertive and demand compliance—you'll be surprised how often that works.

Accept partial delivery. Perhaps your supplier can't deliver all 2,000 widgets called for by the project standard, but can deliver 1,000 on time and the balance within a week or two. You can renegotiate with your customer—perhaps the quantity you can make with 1,000 widgets will satisfy the customer's critical requirement and allow you to meet the rest of the needs on a renegotiated schedule.

xercise #12:

Draw a Tracking Gantt Chart

Using the data in the Project Control Chart below, create a Tracking Gantt Chart from the Gantt Chart on page 255.

Project Control Chart			
Task	**Planned**	**Actual**	**Variance**
A	2	2	0
B	1	2	1
C	2	3	1
D	1	1	0
E	2	1	-1
F	1	1	0
G	1	1	0

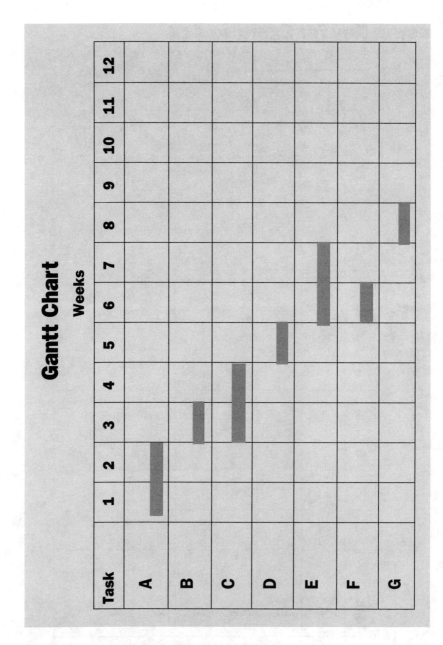

What is the schedule variance of the project? _____

Answer Key for Exercise #12

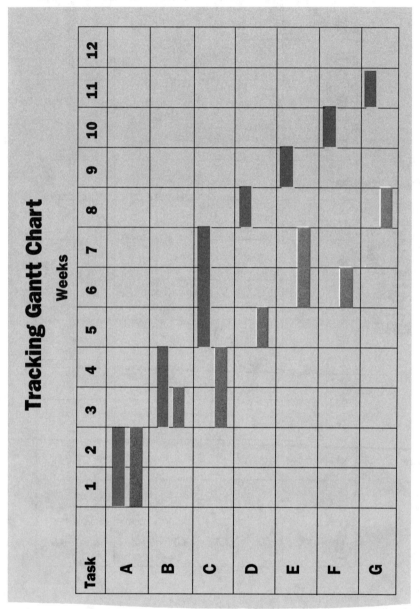

Tracking Gantt Chart
Weeks

Schedule variance is 3 days late (end at day 11 rather than day 8).

Special Techniques for Managing Multiple Projects

12

Managing the Project Portfolio

Many project managers have responsibility for managing multiple, simultaneous projects. A collection of co-managed projects is a *project portfolio,* and there are special techniques for coping with those problems.

Sometimes the individual projects in the portfolio are quite small. You serve as project manager for each individual project as well as for the portfolio as a whole (if they're small enough, you also do technical tasks on each of the projects). Sometimes the projects are individually quite large. In that case, you normally employ separate project managers for the different projects, and you yourself provide overall coordination and executive direction. The difference between being a project manager and a portfolio manager is often additional rank and authority.

Project portfolios are divided into two major categories: independent project portfolios and interdependent project portfolios.

In an *independent project portfolio,* the projects fall under a common management umbrella, but the projects themselves are essentially unrelated. If you manage a construction company, each individual construction project is independent of the others. If one project should fail, the failure has little impact on the other projects in the portfolio (although it might affect your job!). The projects in the portfolio may be similar or dissimilar.

In an *interdependent project portfolio,* the projects are elements in a "super-project" that is aimed at a common outcome. The failure of one project in the portfolio could have a catastrophic impact on the ultimate outcome.

What's the difference, then, between an interdependent project portfolio and a very large project? It's simply a matter of point of view. If your large project has subprojects that you manage individually, you might find it useful to look at the work as a collection of projects as well as a comprehensive project by itself.

All of this leads to the single key to understanding how to make sense of a multiple-project portfolio: *a project and a task are synonymous*. As you learned in the WBS discussion, the difference between a project and a task is perspective: where you stand depends upon where you sit. Tasks, like projects, have the Triple Constraints—they too have goals.

Therefore, the secret of managing project portfolios is to remember that from your perspective, you are managing only one project with multiple (and very large) tasks.

How does this understanding benefit you? It means that you can apply every single technique that works on a single project to the project portfolio. The theory is the same; the methodology is the same. The arithmetic is more complex, and that's the only difference. (And, of course, that's why you might want to use software to assist you.)

You already know a lot about managing multiple projects if you know about managing one project, but this chapter provides some special insights to assist you.

Independent Project Portfolios

Managing independent portfolios resembles the plate-spinning act on Ed Sullivan: your job is to keep all the plates spinning. Wobbling is okay as long as none fall down. Monitor the individual projects and move your attention from one to the other as needed. Prioritize the individual projects based on total value to the organization and portfolio mission. Unlike the Ed Sullivan act, some of your plates might be made of fine china and others of melamine. When faced with a priority, focus on the china and let the melamine fall to the floor.

If a project and a task are the same, then a portfolio and a project are also the same. But keep this in mind: *The driver of the portfolio is not automatically identical to the driver of the individual projects within the portfolio.*

That seems impossible, until you look a little further. On a project/task level, you might have a project with time as the driver. That would imply that time is the driver for each task in the project. But what if a task is noncritical? If it has slack, then time is not the most restrictive constraint. Therefore, the driver of the task is different from the driver of the project.

The same thing can be true of your portfolio. You must develop the portfolio's Triple Constraints and analyze their ranking to determine driver/middle/weak constraint order. This allows you to prioritize the individual projects within the portfolio and make the right strategic decisions, such as how to allocate resources across your projects, in order to optimize the driver.

Because the projects aren't particularly interrelated, use a Gantt Chart approach to track them (see fig. 12.1).

Tip! Sometimes you'll find that a large magnetic status board Gantt Chart is a better tool for multiple project tracking than a computerized one. You can hold staff meetings around it and make a much stronger visual impact. Use appropriate technology to solve your problems, not necessarily high technology.

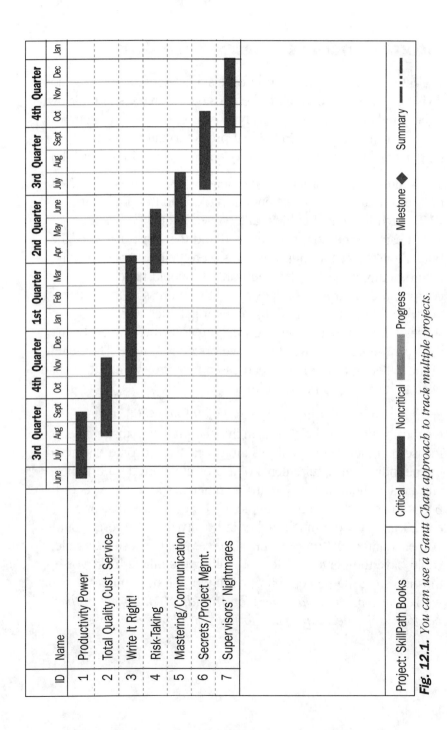

ID	Name	3rd Quarter			4th Quarter			1st Quarter			2nd Quarter			3rd Quarter			4th Quarter			
		June	July	Aug	Sept	Oct	Nov	Dec	Jan	Feb	Mar	Apr	May	June	July	Aug	Sept	Oct	Nov	Dec	Jan
1	Productivity Power																				
2	Total Quality Cust. Service																				
3	Write It Right!																				
4	Risk-Taking																				
5	Mastering/Communication																				
6	Secrets/Project Mgmt.																				
7	Supervisors' Nightmares																				

Project: SkillPath Books   Critical ▬▬ Noncritical ▬▬ Progress ▬▬ Milestone ◆ Summary ▬▬▬

Fig. 12.1. *You can use a Gantt Chart approach to track multiple projects.*

Interdependent Project Portfolios

The interdependent project portfolio is a large project with major divisions important enough to be considered projects in their own right. The key to managing this type of portfolio is to remember that you can't allow any individual project to fail without fundamentally compromising the overall success of the portfolio.

The Smithsonian National Air and Space Museum was a large project, but also an interdependent project portfolio (see fig. 12.2). Each individual exhibit gallery clearly qualified as a project, as did each aircraft that was restored and the construction of the building itself. As the museum plans were being carried out, the failure of any project within the portfolio would have compromised and possibly destroyed the success of the entire portfolio. For example, if all the exhibit galleries were successfully completed, but the building construction had been delayed, the museum wouldn't have opened on time. The quality of the galleries would have been essentially irrelevant if there had been no building to put them in.

From a management point of view, one of your critical responsibilities is to help your individual project managers keep focused on the overall goal. It's all too easy to become distracted by the individual requirements of a project within the portfolio and pursue them in a way that's detrimental to the interests of the portfolio as a whole. For example, if you could see that one exhibit gallery were much higher in quality than the rest, would you encourage that project performance? No, because that gallery could have the perverse effect of making the others look worse, thus lowering the perception of quality of the museum as a whole. *Remember: What is best for an individual project in the portfolio is not necessarily best for the portfolio itself.*

Another key management issue in the interdependent project portfolio is resource allocation. Given the reality that resources are always limited but opportunity is unlimited, you must allocate the resources you have to the projects in your portfolio. To ensure that you meet your most important objectives, you should allocate resources in a two-pass process.

First, identify the minimum acceptable performance level for each project in the portfolio and the resources necessary to achieve that minimum level. Allocate the minimum resource requirements. If you have no more resources, the minimum is now the best you can do.

Second, allocate any remaining resources to achieve maximum portfolio achievement. Don't automatically allocate resources evenly across your projects, because some of your projects don't improve portfolio quality once they have achieved the minimum. For example, in construction no one paints the inside of the drywall, because it doesn't add to the quality of the building as a whole.

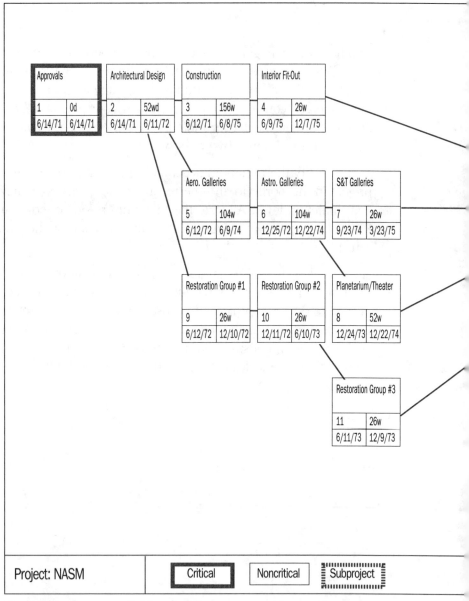

Fig. 12.2. *The creation of the Smithsonian National Air and Space Museum was an example of both a large project and an interdependent project portfolio. This Pert chart gives an idea of the scope and interrelatedness of the work.*

Move-In		Aircraft Installation		Exhibit Installation		Audio-Visual Hookups		Test Systems/Dry Run		Grand Opening	
12	4w	13	8w	14	8w	15	8w	16	4w	17	0d
12/8/75	1/4/76	1/5/76	2/29/76	2/9/76	4/4/76	3/15/76	5/9/76	5/10/76	6/6/76	7/1/76	7/1/76

Milestone   Critical Marked

Resource Scheduling for Multiple Projects

In your study of Gantt Charting, you used a Resource Gantt Chart to show how each project resource was used. (*Tip!* Resources can be people or they can be machines or equipment.) In a multiple project environment, some of your resources may be specialized: they can't do every task in a single project, but they contribute an important element to each project in the portfolio.

One of the hardest operational challenges is to track and allocate resources across multiple projects. The Resource Gantt Chart helps. There's no reason why each task line on the Gantt Chart must come from the same project; in fact, you can easily create a Gantt Chart with each line representing a different project. This keeps track of resources across project lines.

Look at figure 12.3. Here, you are looking at a magazine layout artist who does layout work for a portfolio of magazines. He performs the tasks of paste up, keyline, blueline, and final proof for each of three magazines. Although there is no project-related reason not to overlap tasks, there is a resource reason: the layout artist can only do one job at a time. Notice that resource availability can drive your scheduling process.

What happens if one task goes over schedule? Notice that schedule slippage doesn't just impact the individual project, it spreads across project lines. If you're an individual project manager (say, the editor of one of these magazines), notice that factors in another magazine can impact your production schedule through no fault of your own.

One idea is to build some deliberate resource slack time into the layout artist's schedule: perhaps an empty day each week or so (depending on the level of risk) so that a problem on one task has a limited cascading effect.

Least Resource Scheduling

The principle of *least resource scheduling* is a technique for getting the maximum total work from your available resources.

If you manage subject-related projects in a portfolio, you probably use individual resources across project lines, as shown in the previous section. Those resources are specific in their application: if they are people, they have specific skills; if they are machines, they do specific things. You can't move them around at will; you can only assign them work for which they have the capability.

You normally don't have exactly the same amount of each resource. Identify your *least (scarcest) resource,* that is, the resource used on multiple projects that is in least supply. Schedule all your projects around your scarcest resource to ensure it is used most efficiently.

For example, if the layout artist is your scarcest resource (you have plenty of editors, writers, and other team members), then the greatest number of issues you can publish is limited by the artist's time. If it takes 10 total layout days per magazine issue, and the layout artist works the standard 200 days per year, then the layout artist can do a maximum of 20 individual issues, no matter how many editors you have. Even that number may be high, because it assumes no sick leave, no vacation, and no accidents.

If you have some additional budget authority, what should you spend it on? More editors? No, because more editors won't get more than 20 issues done per year. Add to your least resource first.

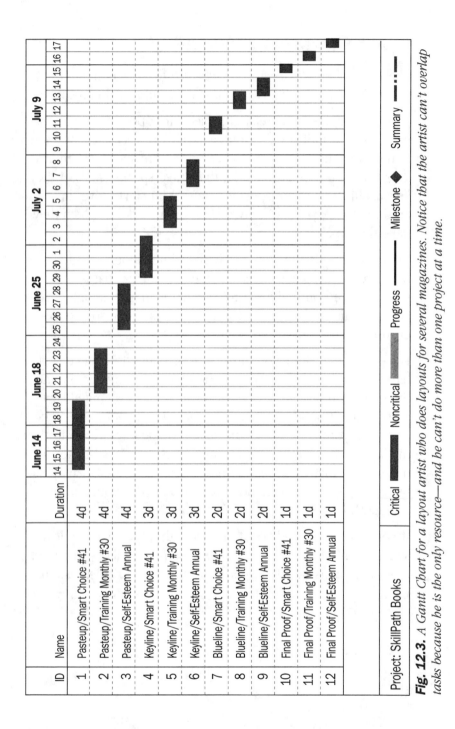

Fig. 12.3. *A Gantt Chart for a layout artist who does layouts for several magazines. Notice that the artist can't overlap tasks because he is the only resource—and be can't do more than one project at a time.*

If you hire a second layout artist, does that mean you can now put out 40 issues per year? It depends on whether two layout artists is still your least resource. Perhaps editors are now more limited.

Whenever you have the power to add resources, add least resources first to achieve maximum production. Manage your least resource carefully, because any time lost or wasted by that resource cuts productivity of the entire portfolio.

Techniques for Managing Priorities and Workflow

Part of achieving success in a multiple-project environment is designing personal control systems. Here are ideas that others have used successfully:

Build your own control systems. Use color-coding for project status reports. Try colored stick-on dots, tinted papers, red dots for priority issues, and other tricks. Put your project tracking information in your personal organizer and calendar your tasks. Use separate clipboards for each project. Keep a project journal/ work diary.

Get and stay organized. Clean your desk at the end of each day. Write a weekly To Do list. Do a Monday morning update. Build quiet time or think time into your work schedule. Buy tools to manage the paper on your desk and learn to use them.

Set and maintain good priorities. Learn to distinguish between importance and urgency. Rank your assignments in this way:

1. By which generates the most profit for the organization

2. By which yields greatest payoff for your time

3. By letting your management decide when neither of the above are compelling.

Speak up. Learn to say "no" when you're overloaded or can't afford to be distracted. When something happens that may jeopardize the project, let the affected people know early. Negotiate. Be assertive.

How to Wrap Up a Project

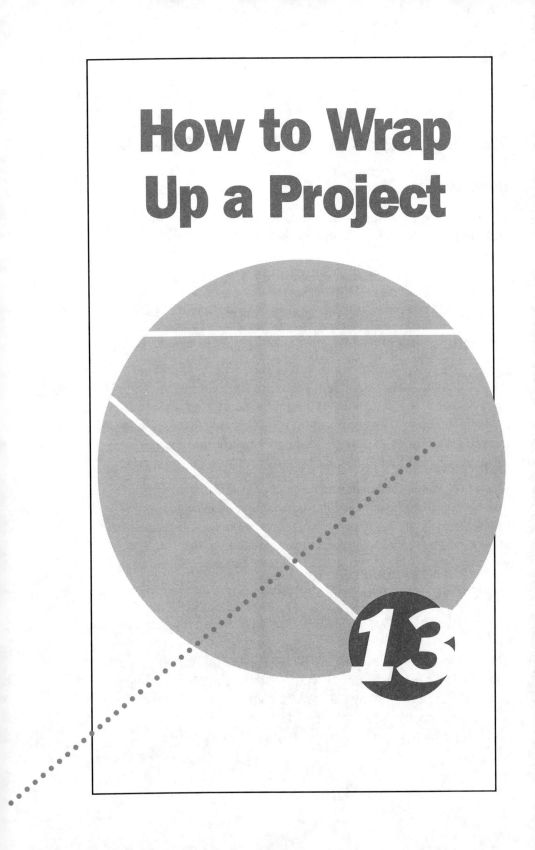

13

The Final Stages of the Project Life Cycle

Complete

When you complete the project, you turn over the end product and then complete certain steps:

- Prepare the paperwork.
- Organize and archive the files.
- Reassign project staff and resources.
- Prepare a wrap-up report.

Earlier, you read about the problem of the 90 percent complete project that has been 90 percent complete for a long time, and no one seems to be able to muster the motivation to get it done. Projects like this suck up opportunity costs, morale dollars, and motivational money merely by existing. They are too expensive for words. Finish them or shoot them—there's no happy medium.

The whole point of managing a project is to finish it, to wrap it up, and to enjoy the fruits of its success. Sometimes projects fester and stagnate. In may workplaces, employees post signs that address the headaches of project management:

> *"When you're up to your rear in alligators, it's hard to remember your original objective was to drain the swamp."*

> *"There is a light at the end of the tunnel. Unfortunately, it's an oncoming train."*

The reasons why projects are hard to complete are varied. Sometimes it's job insecurity: If you finish the project, you might wonder, will the company still need me and my team? Sometimes it's fear of success. Sometimes it's a lack of enthusiasm for the goal. Sometimes it's an inappropriate love of *process*.

Sometimes the remaining tasks on a job are the boring ones: wrapping up the paperwork, assembling the files, writing the final reports. Many project managers hate to do them; they procrastinate. One reason this happens is that these wrap-up tasks are "off-schedule." But don't let them be. If they are part of making the project a complete success, make them tasks, put them in the schedule, and assign them to yourself.

Sometimes the end of a project is difficult because initial expectations were unrealistic. Operating from an impossible plan and budget, some project managers paper over the problem rather than face the facts. When the inevitable crisis arrives, they put the project aside and stall disaster.

If you're going to be an outstanding project manager, make sure that you're fully committed to the outcome. Do whatever it takes to keep your energy and focus high. Your mission is success. Success means completing the project.

Evaluate

Build a mechanism for evaluation into your project. Keep a project journal and record surprises, problems, and options. Hold a "lessons learned" meeting with the project team and brainstorm ideas for the future.

Make sure that the evaluation step is proactive and positive rather than punitive. You don't want to follow the traditional "6 Steps of the Project:"

1. Enthusiasm

2. Disillusionment

3. Panic

4. Search for the Guilty

5. Punishment for the Innocent

6. Praise for Nonparticipants

A good evaluation is never aimed at fault-finding. Try the "liked-best/next-time" approach. Using this approach, you first focus on everything that went right and figure out how to replicate it on your next project. Only after you focus on the positive aspects do you proceed to the "next time" phase. Here you focus on how to make certain tasks even more successful in the future.

Of all the different techniques for gaining excellence and skill as a project manager, none is more important than evaluating every project you complete. You might want to reread this book after you finish your next project to see whether following the ideas more closely would have made a significant difference in that project. Identify skills you might need for the future. Develop an action plan for making yourself a better project manager next time.

Celebrate

Morale is an organizational asset. Take the time to glory in your success. Sit back and look at it. Learn to pat yourself on the back.

Don't overlook the importance of others who contributed to the project. Write letters of appreciation to outstanding team members. Say "thank you" in person. If appropriate, have a party or celebration.

A little creativity goes a long way. At the end of the Smithsonian National Air and Space Museum project, team members were given a certificate that read, "Thank You For Your Significant Service in Opening the National Air and Space Museum." On the bottom of the certificate was a square inch of dry-rotted fabric—it had been removed from the Spirit of St. Louis during refurbishing.

You may not have a memento of that significance to share, but the basic principle works. In other words, examine the circumstances of your project. Is there any memento or souvenir that you can arrange for your team members? It need neither be expensive nor elaborate. It's amazing how much morale you can buy with a little dry-rotted fabric.

You'll need many of your team members again in the future. People like being part of a winning team and having their success celebrated. Celebrating is a powerful tool for raising team morale and making your projects even stronger in the future.

Successful Project Managers

This book began by describing project managers as people who think like project managers. The tools and techniques shared in these pages are ingredients you'll need to achieve, but the most important element is you. By understanding the tools and concepts, building on your strengths, and improving your creativity, you gain the power to succeed.

"Doing it right" requires time and effort, but it's cheaper than doing it over. No matter how hard you plan and anticipate, surprises, problems, and conflict are inevitable. Understanding the political agenda and the motivations of others is always a key.

Your reward for managing an important project successfully is usually another project, even harder and more political than the last one. Whether you consider that a reward or not depends on whether you're a real project manager. There have always been only three routes to career success: do what you love, learn to love what you do, or get the heck out. If you love project management or have simply learned to love project management's results, then you will consider this a reward. If you don't, try to avoid it in the future. There are lots of other opportunities in the world that don't require these skills.

Although the skills of project management take time and effort to hone and manage, that time and effort is richly repaid in easier, smoother, and higher quality projects. You can do it. Good luck.

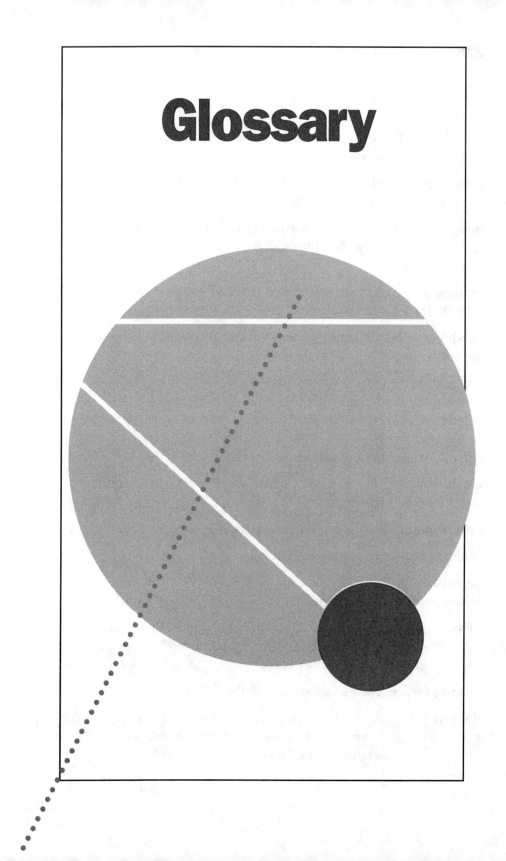

Glossary

actual cost of work performed (ACWP). Actual cost of performing the given task.

budget control chart. A graph that shows cumulative project costs over the life of the project

budgeted cost of work performed (BCWP). The "earned value"—a measure of the dollar value of the work actually performed to date.

budgeted cost of work scheduled (BCWS). Original budget estimate for a given task.

crash cost. The total cost of the resources necessary to achieve the crash time.

crash slope. It is actually two numbers. First, it's the difference between the crash time and the normal time. Second, it's the difference between the crash cost and the normal cost. There can be different points on the crash slope, because there can be different scenarios of resources versus time.

crash time. The fastest time in which a task can be accomplished given unlimited resources.

critical path. The longest full path in a project.

critical task. A task on the critical path.

dependent task. A task that can't begin until one or more predecessor tasks are complete.

driver. The Triple Constraint that drives the project. If you fail to accomplish the driver, the project is a failure, regardless of how well you accomplish the other constraints.

driving forces. Forces that support the solution.

dummy task. The planning technique known as "activity-on-arrow PERT" is an arrow that shows a dependency relationship between two otherwise parallel tasks.

free slack. The amount of time a task can be delayed without delaying the start of the next task.

full path. A sequence that leads from the first task of a project to the final path of the project.

goal. A change that one or more customers desires. Goals can involve cost savings, revenue improvements, work process improvements, saving time, and so on.

independent project portfolio. The projects fall under a common management umbrella, but the projects themselves are essentially unrelated.

interdependent project portfolio. The projects are elements in a "super-project" that is aimed at a common outcome.

lag task. A task that must be shown in the work flow although it has no work associated with it.

least (scarcest) resource. The resource used on multiple projects that is in least supply.

least resource scheduling. A technique for getting the maximum total work from your available resources.

middle constraint. The Triple Constraint that is stronger than the weak constraint and weaker than the driver. It comes in the middle.

milestone task. A task that requires no time or budget but must be shown in the work flow. In a project timeline, a milestone is often shown with a diamond symbol (♦).

negative slack. There isn't enough time (a negative amount of time) to accomplish a task.

noncritical task. A task on any path or path segment that isn't critical.

objective. A written statement of a project, designed to achieve one or more goals.

parallel task. A task that may be performed during the same time frame as other tasks.

path. A sequence of tasks in a dependent order.

path segment. A sequence of tasks in between two internal tasks.

predecessor task. The task that comes immediately before a current task on which the current task depends for its start.

project portfolio. A collection of co-managed projects.

restraining forces. Forces that work against the solution.

schedule variance. Expressed as BCWP minus BCWS, which shows schedule variance in monetary terms.

slack. The extra time available to perform noncritical tasks.

total slack. The amount of time a task can be delayed without delaying the end of the project.

Triple Constraints. The key elements in any project definition. You must fully define and understand the Triple Constraints before you begin to manage any project. The three constraints are Time constraint, Budget constraint, and Performance criteria.

weak constraint. The Triple Constraint that is most flexible and/or least important to achieving your project goal.

Bibliography
and Suggested
Resources

Baker, Sunny, and Kim Baker. *On Time—On Budget: A Step by Step Guide for Managing Any Project*. New York: Prentice Hall, 1992.

Blanchard, Kenneth, and Spencer Johnson. *The One Minute Manager*. New York: Berkley Books, 1983.

Caroselli, Marlene. *Meetings That Work*. Mission, KS: SkillPath Publications, 1992.

Cleland, David I., and William R. King. *Project Management Handbook*. New York: Van Nostrand Reinhold, 1983.

Covey, Stephen R. *The Seven Habits of Highly Effective People*. New York: Simon and Schuster, 1989.

Dawson, Roger. *The Secrets of Power Negotiating* (audio); Chicago: Nightingale-Conant, 1987.

Feder, Michael E. *Taking Charge*. Mission, KS: SkillPath Publications, 1989.

Finkler, Steven A. *The Complete Guide to Finance and Accounting for Nonfinancial Managers*. Englewood Cliffs, NJ: Prentice-Hall, 1983.

Frame, J. Davidson. *Managing Projects in Organizations: How to Make the Best Use of Time, Techniques, and People*. San Francisco: Jossey-Bass, 1987.

Gardner, Reich. *How to Manage Projects* (audio). Mission, KS: SkillPath Publications, 1989.

Gonick, Larry, and Woolcott Smith. *The Cartoon Guide to Statistics*. New York: HarperCollins, 1993.

Gray, Clifford F. *Essentials of Project Management*. New York: Petrocelli Books, 1981.

Haynes, Marion E. *Project Management*. Los Altos, CA: Crisp Publications, 1981.

Imai, Masaaki. *Kaizen: The Key to Japan's Competitive Success.* New York: Random House, 1986.

Kennedy, Marilyn Moates. *Office Politics* (audio); Chicago: Nightingale-Conant, 1989.

Lowery, Gwen. *Managing Projects with Microsoft Project: Version 3.0 for Windows and Macintosh.* New York: Van Nostrand Reinhold, 1992.

Moder, Joseph J. *Project Management With CPM, PERT, and Precedence Diagramming.* New York: Van Nostrand Reinhold, 1983.

Spinner, M. *Elements of Project Management: Plan, Schedule, and Control.* Englewood Cliffs, NJ: Prentice-Hall, 1981.

Temme, Jim. *Managing Multiple Projects, Priorities and Objectives* (audio); Mission, KS: SkillPath Publications, 1990.

Temme, Jim. *Productivity Power.* Mission, KS: SkillPath Publications, 1993.

Towers, Mark. *Dynamic Delegation.* Mission, KS: SkillPath Publications, 1993.

Zinn, Dain. *Project Management* (audio); Chicago: Nightingale-Conant, 1994.

Additional Resources

Project Management Institute, P.O. Box 43, Drexel Hill, PA 19026-3190, (215) 622-1796.

Software Sources. PC Warehouse (800) 367-7080 or MacWarehouse (800) 255-6227.

Index

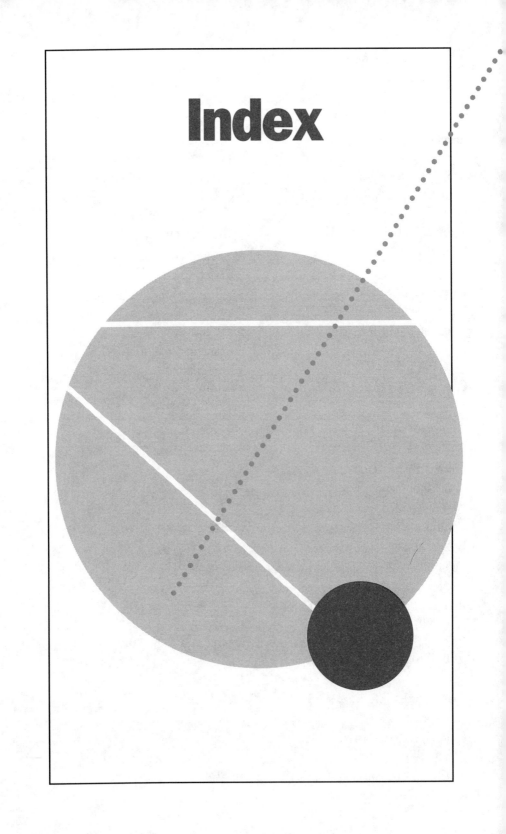

Available From SkillPath Publications

Lifelong Learning Library

Practical Project Management: The Secrets of Managing Any Project on Time and on Budget *by Michael Dobson*

Team Power: How to Build and Grow Successful Teams *by Jim Temme*

Self-Study Sourcebooks

Climbing the Corporate Ladder: What You Need to Know and Do to Be a Promotable Person *by Barbara Pachter and Marjorie Brody*

Coping With Supervisory Nightmares: 12 Common Nightmares of Leadership and What You Can Do About Them *by Michael and Deborah Singer Dobson*

Defeating Procrastination: 52 Fail-Safe Tips for Keeping Time on Your Side *by Marlene Caroselli, Ed.D.*

Discovering Your Purpose *by Ivy Haley*

Going for the Gold: Winning the Gold Medal for Financial Independence *by Lesley D. Bissett, CFP*

Having Something to Say When You Have to Say Something: The Art of Organizing Your Presentation *by Randy Horn*

Info-Flood: How to Swim in a Sea of Information Without Going Under *by Marlene Caroselli, Ed.D.*

The Innovative Secretary *by Marlene Caroselli, Ed.D.*

Letters & Memos: Just Like That! *by Dave Davies*

Mastering the Art of Communication: Your Keys to Developing a More Effective Personal Style *by Michelle Fairfield Poley*

Organized for Success! 95 Tips for Taking Control of Your Time, Your Space, and Your Life *by Nanci McGraw*

A Passion to Lead! How to Develop Your Natural Leadership Ability *by Michael Plumstead*

P.E.R.S.U.A.D.E.: Communication Strategies That Move People to Action *by Marlene Caroselli, Ed.D.*

Productivity Power: 250 Great Ideas for Being More Productive *by Jim Temme*

Promoting Yourself: 50 Ways to Increase Your Prestige, Power, and Paycheck *by Marlene Caroselli, Ed.D.*

Proof Positive: How to Find Errors Before They Embarrass You *by Karen L. Anderson*

Risk-Taking: 50 Ways to Turn Risks Into Rewards *by Marlene Caroselli, Ed.D. and David Harris*

Speak Up and Stand Out: How to Make Effective Presentations *by Nanci McGraw*

Stress Control: How You Can Find Relief From Life's Daily Stress *by Steve Bell*

The Technical Writer's Guide *by Robert McGraw*

Total Quality Customer Service: How to Make It Your Way of Life *by Jim Temme*

Write It Right! A Guide for Clear and Correct Writing *by Richard Andersen and Helene Hinis*

Your Total Communication Image *by Janet Signe Olson, Ph.D.*

Handbooks

The ABC's of Empowered Teams: Building Blocks for Success *by Mark Towers*

Assert Yourself! Developing Power-Packed Communication Skills to Make Your Points Clearly, Confidently, and Persuasively *by Lisa Contini*

Breaking the Ice: How to Improve Your On-the-Spot Communication Skills *by Deborah Shouse*

The Care and Keeping of Customers: A Treasury of Facts, Tips, and Proven Techniques for Keeping Your Customers Coming BACK! *by Roy Lantz*

Challenging Change: Five Steps for Dealing With Change *by Holly DeForest and Mary Steinberg*

Dynamic Delegation: A Manager's Guide for Active Empowerment *by Mark Towers*

Every Woman's Guide to Career Success *by Denise M. Dudley*

Grammar? No Problem! *by Dave Davies*

Great Openings and Closings: 28 Ways to Launch and Land Your Presentations With Punch, Power, and Pizazz *by Mari Pat Varga*

Hiring and Firing: What Every Manager Needs to Know *by Marlene Caroselli, Ed.D. with Laura Wyeth, Ms.Ed.*

How to Be a More Effective Group Communicator: Finding Your Role and Boosting Your Confidence in Group Situations *by Deborah Shouse*

How to Deal With Difficult People *by Paul Friedman*

Learning to Laugh at Work: The Power of Humor in the Workplace *by Robert McGraw*

Making Your Mark: How to Develop a Personal Marketing Plan for Becoming More Visible and More Appreciated at Work *by Deborah Shouse*

Meetings That Work *by Marlene Caroselli, Ed.D.*

The Mentoring Advantage: How to Help Your Career Soar to New Heights *by Pam Grout*

Minding Your Business Manners: Etiquette Tips for Presenting Yourself Professionally in Every Business Situation *by Marjorie Brody and Barbara Pachter*

Misspeller's Guide *by Joel and Ruth Schroeder*

Motivation in the Workplace: How to Motivate Workers to Peak Performance and Productivity *by Barbara Fielder*

NameTags Plus: Games You Can Play When People Don't Know What to Say *by Deborah Shouse*

Networking: How to Creatively Tap Your People Resources *by Colleen Clarke*

New & Improved! 25 Ways to Be More Creative and More Effective *by Pam Grout*

Power Write! A Practical Guide to Words That Work *by Helene Hinis*

The Power of Positivity: Eighty ways to energize your life *by Joel and Ruth Schroeder*

Putting Anger to Work For You *by Ruth and Joel Schroeder*

Reinventing Your Self: 28 Strategies for Coping With Change *by Mark Towers*

Saying "No" to Negativity: How to Manage Negativity in Yourself, Your Boss, and Your Co-Workers *by Zoie Kaye*

The Supervisor's Guide: The Everyday Guide to Coordinating People and Tasks *by Jerry Brown and Denise Dudley, Ph.D.*

Taking Charge: A Personal Guide to Managing Projects and Priorities *by Michal E. Feder*

Treasure Hunt: 10 Stepping Stones to a New and More Confident You! *by Pam Grout*

A Winning Attitude: How to Develop Your Most Important Asset! *by Michelle Fairfield Poley*

For more information, call 1-800-873-7545.

Notes